WEB RESEARCH

WEB RESEARCH

Selecting, Evaluating, and Citing

SECOND EDITION

MARIE L. RADFORD

Rutgers, The State University of New Jersey

SUSAN B. BARNES

Rochester Institute of Technology

LINDA R. BARR

Texas Lutheran University

Boston ■ New York ■ San Francisco
Mexico City ■ Montreal ■ Toronto ■ London ■ Madrid ■ Munich ■ Paris
Hong Kong ■ Singapore ■ Tokyo ■ Cape Town ■ Sydney

Executive Editor: Karon Bowers
Series Editor: Brian Wheel
Series Editorial Assistant: Heather Hawkins
Senior Marketing Manager: Mandee Eckersley
Editorial-Production Service: Omegatype Typography, Inc.
Manufacturing Buyer: JoAnne Sweeney
Composition and Prepress Buyer: Linda Cox
Electronic Composition: Omegatype Typography, Inc.
Cover Administrator: Rebecca Krzyzaniak

For related titles and support materials, visit our online catalog at www.ablongman.com.

Between the time website information is gathered and published, it is not unusual for some sites to have closed. Also, the transcription of URLs can result in typographical errors. The publisher would appreciate notification where these errors occur so that they may be corrected in subsequent editions.

Library of Congress Cataloging-in-Publication Data

Radford, Marie L.
  Web research : selecting, evaluating, and citing / Marie L. Radford, Susan B. Barnes, Linda R. Barr.
    p. cm.
  Includes bibliographical references and index.
  ISBN 0-205-46747-4 (pbk.)
  1. Internet research. 2. Internet searching. 3. Computer network resources—Evaluation. 4. Citation of electronic information resources. I. Barnes, Susan B. II. Barr, Linda R. (Linda Robinson) III. Title.

ZA4228.R33 2006
025.04—dc22

2005045884

Printed in the United States of America

CONTENTS

• •

....

CHAPTER THREE

Content Evaluation   51

....

CHAPTER FOUR

Visual Evaluation   62

CHAPTER FIVE

Copyright Issues and the Web   81

ACKNOWLEDGMENTS

Behind the scenes, there are many people who contribute to the creation of a book. First and foremost, we thank our editor, Brian Wheel, for being patient with the revisions. Additionally, we would like to thank the editorial assistant at Allyn & Bacon/Longman, Heather Hawkins.

Creating a book about the Web requires visuals. Once again, we are very fortunate to have the artistic talent of John Terhorst who created the Dot Com character for the first edition and who has drawn many additional illustrations of exceptional quality for this edition. Additionally, we would like to thank all of the individuals, companies, and organizations that allowed us to use screen captures of their websites, including the Library of Congress, Elizabeth Lane Lawley, Texas Luthern University, Rochester Institute of Technology (RIT), Google, Yahoo!, Dogpile, Danny Schechter, and mediachannel.

In addition to the people mentioned above, each of us has her own group of people to thank. Marie L. Radford thanks her husband Gary P. Radford for his gentle reassurance, patience, encouragement, and for his help with the index. She also extends heartfelt thanks to Denise A. Feder, MLIS student at Rutgers University, SCILS, for editorial assistance and for her searching expertise in updating chapter bibliographies. Susan B. Barnes would like to thank the librarians at RIT, Margaret Bartlett, Linda Coppola, and Chan McKenzie, along with Bob Finnerty. She also would like to acknowledge the help of RIT graduate assistant John Erhardt for his help researching sections of this text. Linda Robinson Barr thanks her parents for reading drafts and for their excitement about the project. She would also like to thank her husband, John Brooks-Barr, for his extra set of eyes.

Finally, we would like to thank all of the reviewers, who provided excellent suggestions for the second edition of this text.

● ●

CHAPTER 1

Using the Web
as a Research Tool

Where is the first place you go to search for information when you get a research assignment? If you are like most college students your first step is most likely to be to reach for your computer keyboard and to search the Web using a favorite search engine like Google (www.google.com). There is no doubt that you have an incredible range of information resources and services available through the World Wide Web (WWW or Web). Since 1993, the Web, a vast interconnected system of global information networks, has been accessible through Internet graphical **browsers,** such as Microsoft Internet Explorer and Netscape Navigator, to help students with research for course assignments. However, much information found on the web is not reliable and it is important for you to sharpen your searching and evaluation skills.

WHAT THIS BOOK *IS* AND *IS NOT*

This book is designed to help you become web savvy—both efficient and effective in using the Web to find the right quantity and highest-quality information you need for your course work and academic assignments. This book is *not* designed to help you find recreational information such as MP3s, the latest concert dates for your favorite rock band, or games.

As you probably are already aware, you can waste valuable study time and quickly become frustrated chasing around cyberspace, unable to zero in on the right website for your research. Before you know it, time quickly slips away while you search through pages full of links to potentially useful web pages, some of which seem to take forever to download. In the end, you are no closer to completing your assignment. This book gives you practical tips on how to find the information you need quickly and painlessly; on how to get help from virtual libraries and Ask-A-Librarian services when you hit a dead end; on how to choose search engines, subject directories, portals, and metasites; and especially on how to evaluate the information that you find. In addition, you can learn how to avoid plagiarism or violating copyright by properly citing web resources in papers and other assignments.

Now, for some basic information, followed by some good news and (yes, unfortunately) some bad news about searching the Web.

THE ROCK-BOTTOM BASICS

On a short deadline? Web resources are instantly available to help you with class assignments. Web pages and databases provide many different types of valuable information, including:

- Facts
- Statistics
- Full-text journal and newspaper articles
- Library holdings
- U.S. and global government information
- Biographical information
- Dictionaries, encyclopedias, almanacs, and handbooks
- Quotations
- Graphics and photographic images
- Directories
- Audio and videoclips

- E-books and e-journals
- Maps and geographical information
- Stock quotes and company information
- First person accounts and opinion pieces
- Scholarly articles and papers
- Online library catalogs of books, journals, and other media

Some Basic Terminology

HTML. HTML **(hypertext markup language)** allows information on web pages to be easily accessed and displayed.

URL. Each web page is located by a URL **(uniform resource locator),** which usually begins with http:// and which you can type into your browser in the location box at the top.

Hyperlinks. **Hyperlinks** quickly connect you to other web pages, databases, and files. They are easily recognized and activated by text highlighted with color, underlining, or graphic buttons.

See the Glossary in the back of the book for additional definitions of terms that appear in **bold** type.

Good News!

Web information is easy to download to a **Flash Drive** (a.k.a. USB drive) or disk or cut and paste into your word processing program. This information can be used for taking notes, writing papers, and preparing oral reports. A variety of **search engines,** specialized subject directories, portals, and **metasites** are available to help you find your way to the best quality information the Web has to offer. The Web can provide a much more efficient and effective way to search traditional resources, such as newspapers and journals. The Web offers the following advantages, according to Berkman (2000):

- **Speed.** Doing web research can be quicker than doing research using paper sources.

- **Timeliness.** Web resources can be more up to date than print materials.
- **Multimedia.** The Web includes audio, video, and graphics.
- **Hyperlinks.** With just a click you can move quickly to related websites.

A steadily increasing number of primary sources (e.g., government documents, speeches, letters, diaries, etc.) have become available through the Web. More authoritative reference sources (e.g., the *Encyclopædia Britannica*, www.britannica.com) are providing web access to their products, for a subscription fee. Others, like *Merriam-Webster's Online Dictionary and Thesaurus* (www.m-w.com), have free as well as fee-based versions. These free sources are usually supported through web advertisements. Most universities are purchasing subscriptions to fee-based information services (e.g., ProQuest or EBSCOhost, which index high-quality full-text journal and newspaper articles on a variety of topics) for student use. You can often use these services both on and off campus through your university library home page.

Bad News! (But Don't Panic)

Although using the Web has its pitfalls and obstacles, the upcoming chapters of this book will help enable you to steer clear. Table 1.1 offers 10 essentials for doing research on the Web.

Information Overload! The vastness of the Web is both a plus and a minus. About 99.99 percent of web resources are useless for obtaining serious research for class assignments. How do you find just the right piece of information you are looking for in billions of web pages?

Yee Haw! The WWW Is the Wild Wild Web! Although billions of web pages are packed full of information, no one is in charge of quality control. How do you know whether the web page you are using to write your research paper is the authoritative real deal or is written by someone's kid sister? Web pages are not permanent; they have a habit of being here today and gone tomorrow.

∙∙

TABLE 1.1   Ten Essentials for Using the Web for Research

∙∙

THE ESSENTIALS	HERE'S MORE INFORMATION	WHAT TO DO
1. Your first stop is your library's home page.	Librarians at your campus have located and organized web and other online resources that are most likely to be of value to *you.* The library home page is a great place to start research for any project. Ask-a-Librarian services can provide online help (See Ch. 2).	Check it out! Go to your library's home page and click on "library" or "academics" to find your library's URL or call or visit the reference desk. Need help in navigating? Ask.
2. The Web is big, really, really big!	Any given search engine is only searching a *fraction* of the Web.	Use several search engines, or a **meta–search engine.**
3. Search engines have different features.	These unique features allow you to combine terms, search word variations, search phrases, search different parts of the Web (e.g., Usenet groups, etc.).	Use Help features (also, Search Tips, Power Searching, or Advanced Searching) when using unfamiliar search engines or when using a favorite search engine, because these engines are always being fine tuned.
4. For best results, combine terms when searching the Web.	**Boolean operators,** such as **AND, OR, NOT,** can reduce the number of unrelated or unwanted websites you retrieve (also known as **false hits**) and increase **precision.**	Always use Boolean operators. Check Help features for the search engine to see how they are used. For example, some search engines use the + sign instead of typing *AND.*
5. Search engines only search words *not* concepts.	When you enter in the word *Java,* for example, the search engine looks for that *exact term.* It cannot tell the difference between *Java* (the programming language), *Java* (the country), or *Java* (the slang term for coffee).	Combine terms for better results. For example, use the words *Java AND Indonesia* for information on the country.

(continued)

TABLE 1.1   (continued)

THE ESSENTIALS	HERE'S MORE INFORMATION	WHAT TO DO
6. Search engines have different ways to determine **relevance** and order of output (that is, which pages appear first, second, etc.).	The search engine may simply count the number of times your term appears. However, other criteria can be used.	Check Help to find out how relevance is determined. Use meta-sites chosen by subject experts to cut down on commercial site (.com) retrieval.
7. GIGO stands for Garbage In, Garbage Out.	GIGO means that just because something is on the Web, that does not make it true. Web content may be inaccurate if mistakes are made when inputting information, or if web page developers are careless or uninformed.	Be aware of the authority of the web page author. Verify web information using another resource if possible. See Chapter 3 for more help in evaluating web content.
8. Let the searcher beware! *No one* edits web content.	Unlike this book or your textbooks, no editorial team is checking facts and verifying information on the Web.

Anyone, repeat *anyone,* can put *anything* on the Web. | Be critical of web content and verify information. See Chapter 3 for more help in evaluating web content. |
| 9. Know what you are searching. | Browsers search the entire Web to retrieve the page that matches the exact URL you enter. Search engines index and search only a small portion of the Web. Some **meta–search engines** search the output of several search engines. If you are searching an online library catalog, or a subscription database from your library's home page (e.g., ProQuest or EBSCO), you are only searching the contents of that database, not the Web at all. | Think before you search! Check search engine Help. Some search engines allow you to search specific portions of the Web (such as Usenets) or by **extensions** or **domain names** (e.g., .com or .gov). |

TABLE 1.1   **(continued)**

THE ESSENTIALS	HERE'S MORE INFORMATION	WHAT TO DO
10. Know your limitations.	Don't assume that you are a super searcher. Even if you have done lots of web searching, new search engines and new resources are becoming available every day, and familiar ones may have changed overnight.	Be open to learning more about searching the Web! Don't be satisfied with the first site you find. Look for quality information. Compare results, don't settle for less.

Search Engine Overload! So many search engines and metasites are available, how do you know which one to use? How do you best use a variety of basic and advanced features of search engines to find quickly what you need? Does your habit of always (and only!) using one search engine (e.g., Google or Yahoo!) for class assignments provide the best results?

Advertisement Overload! The advertisements on search engines and reference resources can be really annoying. How can you avoid them?

Caution! Plagiarism Potential. Cite Your Site! Because the information from the Web is so easy to download or cut and paste into your word processor when writing papers, it is easy to forget to cite your sources or to keep track of direct quotes. (For more information on **plagiarism,** see Chapter 5.)

TIP

Where do you think that the savviest web searchers on your campus are to be found? Give up? They are in your campus library! That's right! Your *librarians,* easily found at the reference desk, are deeply involved in web searching, evaluation of resources, and selecting the highest quality websites for you to easily find on your library's home page. Some even have titles such as *cybrarian* or *library web developer.* Check your library's home page to see if they offer email or chat Ask-A-Librarian services that you can access from on or off campus. Don't forget that you can usually phone the library reference desk for immediate help until closing time.

IDENTIFYING WEBSITES

When evaluating websites, it is helpful first to identify the type of site that you are viewing. Websites can be placed into six basic categories:

- Advocacy
- Business
- Informational
- News
- Personal
- Entertainment

Sometimes you can tell the type of site by looking at the web address, or uniform resource locator (URL). The URL is the address of the website. URLs contain information about where the file is located. Each web page has its own unique URL. The web address includes the **hypertext transport protocol (http),** the name of the server the page is located on (also called the **domain name**), the path or location of the page, and the name of the individual page. For example, all these bits of information are contained in the following URL: www.server.edu/path/file_name.html.

Websites are created for a variety of different reasons (see Table 1.2). Identifying the purpose of the site helps you evaluate the credibility of the site. For example, a site designed to promote a product, as a television commercial does, will only say good things about it. Similarly, advocacy sites are created to convince you to support their cause. Knowing the point of view expressed by the site or its bias is important in determining the credibility of information.

Advocacy Sites.   Advocacy sites are created to influence public opinion or to encourage activism. The individuals, groups, or organizations that run these sites often attempt to increase membership in the organization. Examples include websites for the Democratic (www.democrats.org) and Republican (www.rnc.org) parties, the American Cancer Society (www.cancer.org), and the American Civil Liberties Union (www.aclu.org).

TIP

Disappearing Links:
What Happens if the URL (Link) You Go to Is Gone?

The Web is a fluid entity and links do move or change names. Sometimes they still exist but under a different URL; sometimes, unfortunately, they are truly gone and do not exist any more. If the web page

∙∙∙

TABLE 1.2   Types of Websites

∙∙∙

TYPE	PURPOSE	URL ADDRESS
Advocacy	To influence public opinion To promote a cause To promote a nonprofit organization	Frequently ends in .org
Business	To promote a product or service	Frequently ends in .com
Informational	To provide factual information	Variety of endings, especially .edu and .org
News	To provide information about local, regional, national, or international news	Frequently ends in .com
Personal	To fulfill a variety of reasons for an individual	Variety of endings, especially .com and .edu
Entertainment	To provide enjoyment	Variety of endings

author is a good egg, he/she will put a "redirector" which, when you go to the old site, will direct you to the new URL. But, if not, there are ways to hunt a bit more to find the "missing" link you know used to be there.

- If you have the title of the web page—that is, the information that shows in the top bar of the browser—then use a search engine such as Google and type in the title inside double quotes. For example, in looking for a web page that existed at one time with the title "History of Montessori," go to Google and type that in, including the quotes. You can even go to Google's advanced search option and ask it to only search the titles.

- If you have the URL, but when you type that into your location bar, you get a 404 error or similar error, try cutting off part of the URL. For example, if the URL was www.montessori-intl.org/history.html but there's an error, take off the "/history.html" which will get you, hopefully, to the main site. From that point, see if you can surf around to find the history of Montessori from a differently named page.

Business Sites.   Business sites are constructed to promote a product or service. These sites may offer online sales catalogs, provide product documentation, distribute press releases and information about the company, offer electronic services, and provide customer support. Business sites generally have a marketing orientation and they may attempt to collect information from web users. Examples are Amazon (www.amazon.com) and Barnes and Noble (www.bn.com).

Informational Sites.   Informational sites are built to provide factual information such as government research reports, census data, transportation schedules, course schedules, and encyclopedia information. A variety of different information sites include everything from concert schedules to government databases. Examples include websites for your college or university, *Merriam-Webster's Online Dictionary and Thesaurus* (www.m-w.com), Fedstats (www.fedstats.gov), and the Library of Congress site (www.loc.gov) (see Figure 1.1).

News Sites.   News sites are often developed by traditional companies, including media formats such as newspapers, magazines, radio stations, television, and books. These websites often parallel the more traditional medium that they represent. For example, the CNN site has video and audioclips from its television station. Your understanding of the traditional medium sponsoring the site can help you determine its credibility. Examples include *The New York Times* (www.nytimes.com), Cable News Network (www.cnn.com), and CNET (www.news.com).

Personal Sites.   Personal sites are designed by individuals for many reasons, including shameless self-promotion, presenting an online resume or portfolio, sharing creative talents such as illustration or writing, providing personal information about a family or personal activities, or providing information about a topic of interest. An example of a personal website is Marie L. Radford's site, which is located at www.scils.rutgers.edu/~mradford (see Figure 1.2).

Entertainment Sites.   Entertainment sites are established to provide enjoyment to users. Entertainment sites may participate in producing parodies that satirize other websites. For example, www.whitehouse.net is a parody of the original White House site, located at www.whitehouse.gov. Other entertainment websites provide games, jokes, fan information, chat, and movie clips. Many of these entertainment sites provide links to related shopping sites.

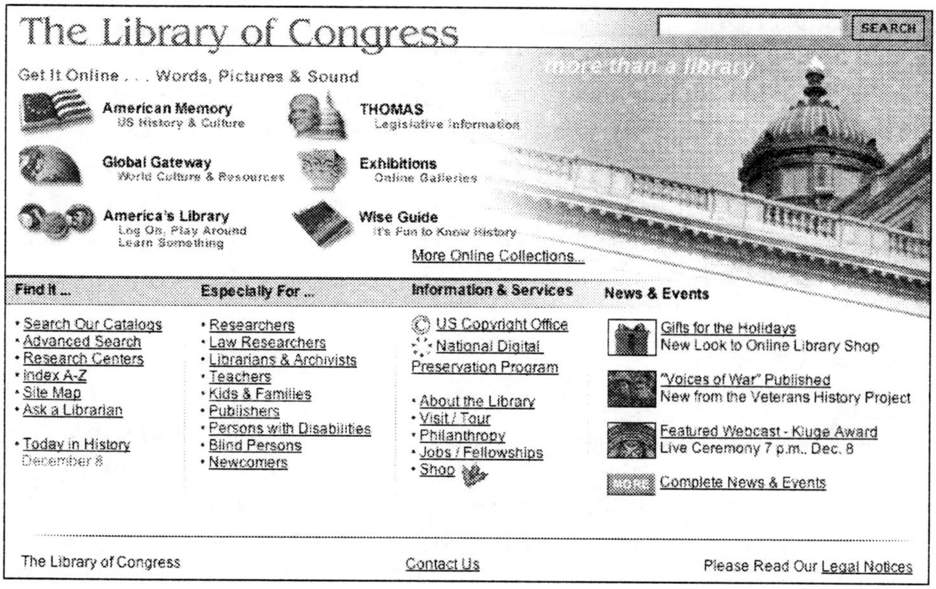

FIGURE 1.1 The Library of Congress website is an informational site that contains text, photographs, maps, graphics, moving images, and other American documents.

Reprinted with permission from the Library of Congress (www.loc.gov).

Marie L. Radford and Joe Thompson of Maryland Ask Us Now! at the RUSA Reference Research Forum, ALA, Orlando, June 2004.

FIGURE 1.2 Marie L. Radford's site is an example of a personal website. She also uses tables to organize elements on the page (see Chapter 4) (www.scils.rutgers.edu/~mradford).

Reprinted with permission from Marie L. Radford.

Many of the sites on the Internet are created for recreational rather than informational purposes. Commercial sites place key words in their titles to attract search engine hits and users. Additionally, commercial search engines make money by collecting advertising revenues. When using the Web as an information source, you could end up with a mixture of many different types of sites.

Did you know that commercial sites (.com sites) often pay search engines to have their sites retrieved first? Of the major search engines, only Google separates paid sites in the results list. Commercial sites (such as beer companies) that want to attract young men to their web pages also may include hot words such as *sex* on their sites so that surfers retrieve them when doing "extracurricular" research.

WEB LOGS OR BLOGS

Blogs (short for web logs) have quickly proliferated on the Web since their origins in the late 1990s. These online, interactive diaries provide "bloggers" (a person who writes a blog) and their readers with an opportunity to share information and points of view on a vast array of topics from the mundane to the most critical news issues. The most popular bloggers site is www.blogger .com owned by Google. The most notable of the "do it yourself blogging tools [that] became available in mid-1999," blogger.com enabled people to easily create blogs that now number in the millions (Williams & Jacobs, 2004, p. 232). Examples of blogs can be found in Figure 1.3 and Figure 4.1 (see p. 66).

To find a blog on just about any topic, you can use two directories:

- Blogwise (www.blogwise.com) indexes 14,000 blogs; or
- Blogarama (www.blogarama.com) indexes 1,000 blogs.

Also, you can try a search engine like Icerocket (www.icerocket.com) that allows you to search blog content.

When doing serious research, you should be aware that there are pros and cons for using information found on a blog. Use blogs for finding:

- Firsthand accounts of events
- Opinions on current topics and news stories

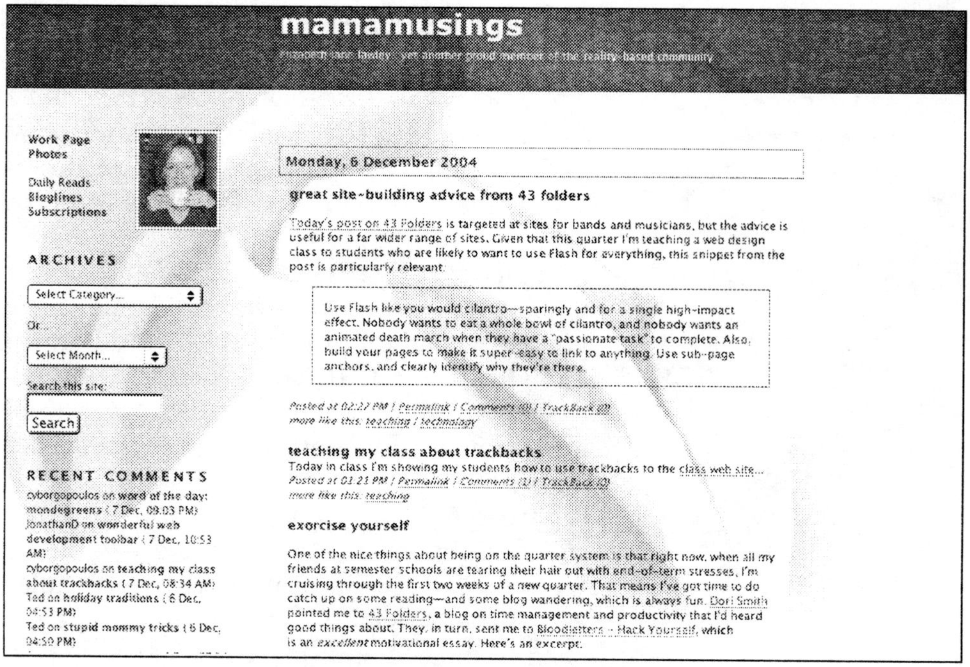

FIGURE 1.3 Mamamusings is a blog that is managed by Elizabeth Lane Lawley. Frequently, this blog discusses the issues of blogging itself.

CC Elizabeth Lane Lawley (www.mamamusings.net).

- Colorful quotations to liven a paper or oral report
- Up-to-the-minute information on breaking news (some are updated every 15 minutes)

Caution when using blog information for assignments:

- There are no editors or fact checkers to confirm the content of blogs.
- Information may be biased or incorrect, so verify all information.
- Opinions are not facts; be sure to label opinions as such.
- Anyone can build a blog; check credentials, do not assume just because a person has a blog that they are subject authorities!

According to Barbara Kaye (2005) information seeking and media checking is one of the primary reasons why people use blogs. It appears certain that blogs are no passing fad and that their use is steadily increasing. So the bottom line here is to consider blogs as one possible source of information, but be aware of the limitations of blogs and verify all information that you plan to cite as fact not opinion.

IDENTIFYING MISINFORMATION
AND HATE SPEECH SITES

Caution was advised when using information found on blogs and the importance of recognizing the difference between opinion and fact. This section discusses the topic of hate speech and deliberate **misinformation** planted on the Web that may masquerade as fact, making it necessary for you to be doubly cautious. As you know, anyone who has a computer, some basic knowledge of HTML, and a little free time, can put up their own website. Thus there is a great deal of misinformation floating around in cyberspace. The Web also makes it easy for a person or organization that sets out to spread myths, partial truths, and outright lies to do so, spreading misinformation like a highly contagious virus. In fact, misinformation is so prevalent on the Web that even some professional journalists, who have been trained to spot inaccuracies, have been caught spreading it by mistake!

You must be especially critical of sites that may contain **hate speech.** Hate speech is making racist or discriminatory comments on the basis of race, gender, origin, disability, or sexual orientation. Although these messages are designed to intimidate others, in the United States, the First Amendment protects everyone's right to free speech, even those who spread hate speech. In contrast to other media with editors and other gatekeepers, hate speech can thrive on the Web. For instance, those who deny that the Holocaust was real can publish their ideas as widely as their hardware and software will allow.

Why the Web Is Filled with Misinformation

Here are some of the reasons why the Web contains incorrect information:

- Hardware and software can damage, corrupt, and fragment data.
- There is no central authority for the Web, so scholarly misconduct or any other flaws can be quickly circulated.
- Data is malleable, which enables pranksters to access and change data.
- Misinformation in a printed format can be easily transferred to the Web.

- To err is human; sometimes people inadvertently make mistakes.
- Misconduct occurs when people deliberately transmit flawed information, such as jokes and pranks.
- Statements can be removed from their original context, which can change an author's intent.
- Hypertext hopping readers may miss relevant pieces of information.
- Sometimes in the name of currency, information is put on the Web quickly without properly checking information sources.
- Increasing numbers of sites and blogs are biased toward a particular point-of-view.

(See Fitzgerald, 1997 for a more detailed description of misinformation).

How to Deal with Hate Speech and Misinformation

When confronted with a site that you think may contain hate speech, check the authority of the site's author or sponsoring organization very carefully. Credibility can be an issue. Professors with strong academic credentials have developed some hate speech sites, so an author may seem legitimate. What to do? Look for discrepancies, inconsistencies, and contradictions. Look for strong language and claims that are unsupported by research. One reason why hate speech can be difficult to detect is because it can appear to be credible.

Hardware, software, human error, and pranksters all contribute to misinformation being placed on the Web. Here are some additional critical thinking tools to help you when navigating the Internet:

- Use your critical awareness whenever you engage in Internet interaction.
- When researching a subject, try to establish some prior knowledge about the topic through wide browsing, reading, and searching.
- Always try to look for the difference between facts and opinions.
- Identify the arguments and evaluate them.
- Compare and contrast information from different websites, sources, and search engines.
- Check the reliability of the sources by looking for inconsistencies in the facts and statistics.

One way to check the reliability of a web source is to Google (www .google.com) the author or organization to find additional information.

WHEN TO USE THE WEB FOR RESEARCH

Now that you know the essentials for using the Web for researching class assignments, let's look at the types of assignments you might have and when you should use the Web (see Table 1.3).

- Rather than operating with a knee-jerk reaction to reach for the mouse or type in Google.com every time you have to look up a fact or write a paper, it is smart to know when web resources can help and when to go someplace else.
- As previously noted, your library home page can be a great starting point for entering into web research (see Figure 1.4). Table 1.3 has been provided to help you become more discriminating when using the Web.

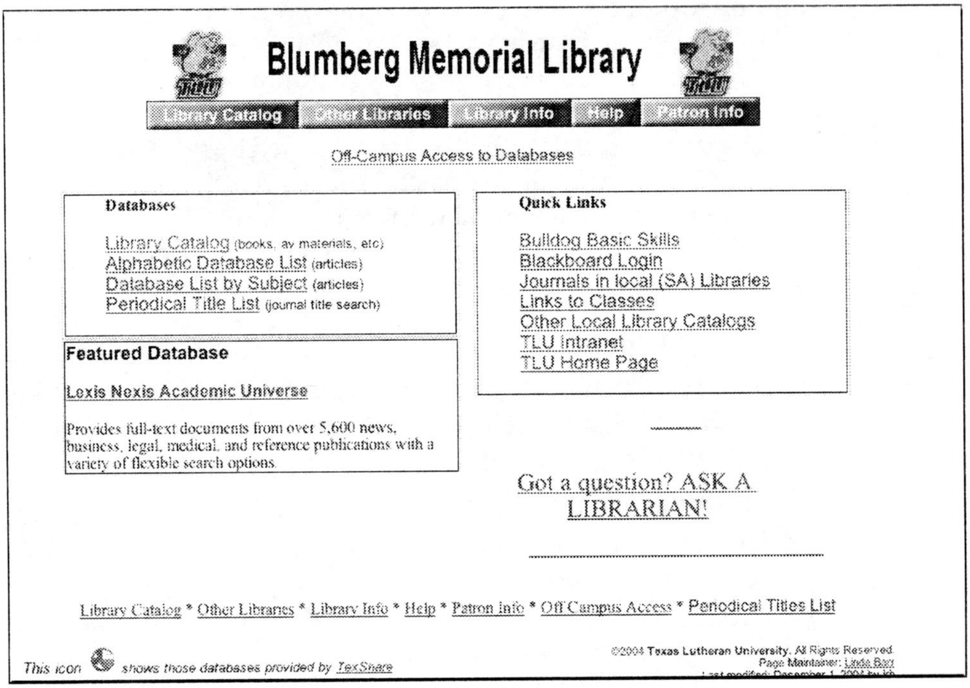

FIGURE 1.4   Some of the best information on the Web can be found by using your university library site.

Reprinted with permission from the Blumberg Memorial Library, Texas Lutheran University (bulldogs.tlu.edu).

> "It is shocking, but sometimes you just have to get dressed, leave the dorm room, and head for the library!"

TABLE 1.3   When to Use the Web for Assignments

ASSIGNMENT	USE THE WEB	USE ANOTHER RESOURCE
Find a fact.	Try the ready reference sites listed on p. 22.	Finding facts on the Web can be a time-consuming task. It is sometimes quicker to go to the library and look up facts. One site to try is Research-It! (www.iTools.com). This site searches many individual web reference sources for facts.
Find a statistic.	Try the government, legal, statistical, U.S., and world resources found on pp. 23–24.	Ditto! But you can find authoritative statistical sources on the Web such as the *Information Please Almanac* (www.info please.com) and FedStats (www.fedstats.gov). See pp. 22–25 for a list.
Build a reference list on a topic (using books and journal articles).	Books—your library's online catalog Journals—Use online journal indexes on your topic at your library home page. You can also use Google Scholar (www .google.com) to find citations and abstracts of scholarly books and articles, although it is not as complete as your library's online catalog and indexes. It also does not provide many full text articles.	You can also use bibliographies found at the end of chapters in your textbook like those found in this book.

(continued)

∙∙∙

TABLE 1.3   (continued)

∙∙∙

ASSIGNMENT	USE THE WEB	USE ANOTHER RESOURCE
Collect general background information for a research paper or oral report.	Use a search engine. The Web can provide basic information on just about any topic. Caution! Don't accept information as fact from commercial sites (.com). Verify using another source when possible.	Use library print or online resources, such as current encyclopedias. Your library has both general and subject encyclopedias.
Write a research paper or oral report using scholarly journals (refereed or juried).	Use journal indexes on your topic at your library home page. But it is rare to find full-text journal articles using a web search engine.	
Write a research paper or oral report using books.	Use your library's online catalog, which contains all the books your library owns.	
Check book citations (or complete a partial citation).	Use your library's online catalog. Use Amazon (www.amazon.com) or Barnes and Noble (www.bn.com).	Call or visit the library reference desk if you cannot find a complete citation.
Research a current event.	Many free websites offer news. Caution! Make sure you are using an authoritative source such as *The New York Times* website (www.nytimes. com). See p. 25 for a list.	
Investigate a controversial topic.	Government sites offer easily accessible information on legislation, such as gun control bills. See Thomas (thomas.loc.gov), for example. Proceed with caution! Many websites and blogs on controversial topics are *largely* opinion, not fact.	

. . . .

TABLE 1.3 (continued)

. . . .

ASSIGNMENT	USE THE WEB	USE ANOTHER RESOURCE
Gather general biographical information.	Some traditional print biographical resources, such as *Current Biography,* are now available online. Check with your library to see what biographical databases are available to you. Use authoritative biographical sites such as those listed on p. 22.	Use library print resources. Any biographical information found through search engines should be verified.
Gather literary biographical information.	Check the library home page to see whether your library has an online resource for this area (e.g., *GALE's Biography Resource Center*).	If your library home page does not have an online resource, go to the library and ask for help. Again, verify any information found through search engines.
Research books.	Use your library's online catalog.	For most books you still have to go to the library. Exceptions include digitized books for which copyright has expired, for example Bartleby (www.bartleby.com) and electronic libraries of e-books, such as netLibrary if your library subscribes.
Present images, pictures, graphs, and tables.	Use a search engine. Increasing numbers of graphics are available on the Web. Caution! You may not be able to download or print out to your satisfaction.	
Interpret a poem or passage.	Use a search engine for background information. Check your library's site for indexes like MLA (Modern Language Association) or *Gale's Literary Resource Center.*	You can find some literary criticism on the Web, but it is more easily found at the library.

(continued)

TABLE 1.3   (continued)

ASSIGNMENT	USE THE WEB	USE ANOTHER RESOURCE
Find a mathematical or chemical formula.		This information can be difficult to find on the Web; use library resources.
Find demographic information.	Most states and many countries have demographic information posted on their websites. Some data is outdated, so verify all dates. Also check federal and foreign government sites (see pp. 23–24 for a list).	Some demographic data is very difficult to find on the Web and may require the help of a librarian.
Obtain company information.	Subscription websites such as Hoovers Online (www.hoovers.com) and Lexis-Nexis (www.lexis-nexis.com) have excellent information. However, they are not free and your library must subscribe.	Caution! You can find some company information at company websites, but it is good to check the library to verify information.
Obtain legislative information.	The Library of Congress supports Thomas (thomas.loc.gov), a great site that provides current and authoritative information on legislation and laws.	
Obtain medical information.	Use web resources with caution! Make sure you verify medical information found on the Web and are searching an authoritative site such as the American Cancer Society (www.cancer.org).	
View maps.	Several good websites exist for maps (see p. 24 for a list). Caution! Some web maps may be out of date.	

SUMMARY
....

In this chapter you read about

- The rock-bottom basics of web searching, including

  Types of information found on the Web

  Some basic terminology

  Good news about searching the Web for assignments

  Bad news about web searching and some words of caution

  Ten essentials for using the Web for research

- Different types of websites, including

  Advocacy

  Business

  Informational

  News

  Personal

  Entertainment

- How to find and when to use blogs for research
- How to recognize and avoid hate speech sites
- When to use the Web for assignments

  Using your library's home page to find books, journal articles, and complete citation information

  Using web search engines to find current events, images, pictures, graphs, tables, some demographic information, and general background information on most topics

  Using print or online resources from the library to find facts, statistics, literary biographical information, and to verify information found on the Web

You now have a good idea of the basics of using the Web for research. In the following chapters, your comfort level will rise as you discover more about the different types of websites, how to evaluate the content on sites, and how to deal with sticky ethical and copyright issues.

NOTHING BUT THE BEST
GREAT FREE WEBSITES FOR RESEARCH

Ready Reference: Fact Finders, Dictionaries, and Encyclopedias

Acronym Finder
www.acronymfinder.com

AskOxford.com
www.askoxford.com

Babel Fish Translation
www.babelfish.altavista.com/tr

Bartlett's Familiar Quotations
www.bartleby.com

Information Please (also includes Sports
Almanac, Entertainment Almanac,
Columbia Encyclopedia, and
Information Please Dictionary)
www.infoplease.com

Medical Dictionary
www.medterms.com

**Merriam-Webster's Online Dictionary
& Thesaurus**
www.m-w.com

Merck Manual of Diagnosis and Therapy
(medical information, diseases)
www.merck.com/pubs/mmanual

Old Farmer's Almanac
www.almanac.com

One Look Dictionaries
www.onelook.com

Research-It!
www.iTools.com

Roget's Thesaurus
www.thesaurus.com

Wikipedia: The Free Encylopedia
en.wikipedia.org

Biographical Information

Biography.com
www.biography.com/search

Lives, the Biography Resource
www.amillionlives.com

Nobel Prize Winners
www.nobelprize.org

Rulers
www.rulers.org

Saints and Angels
saints.catholic.org

Directories: People, Places, Addresses

AT&T Any Who
www.anywho.com

Bigfoot
www.bigfoot.com

City Search
www.citysearch.com

411.com
www.411.com

Infospace
www.infospace.com

**SBC Online National Yellow
Pages Directory**
www.smartpages.com

Switchboard
www.switchboard.com

Who Where
www.whowhere.com

WorldPages
www.worldpages.com

Financial and Corporate Sources

Big Charts
bigcharts.marketwatch.com

CI: Corporate Information
www.corporateinformation.com

Hoovers (company research)
www.hoovers.com

MSNBC
www.msnbc.com

Thomas Register
www.thomasnet.com

Wall Street Journal Online
www.wsj.com

Yahoo Business News
news.yahoo.com

Government, Legal, Statistical, US and World Resources

American Memory (maps, journals, photos, sound, and video on U.S. history)
memory.loc.gov

Board of Governors of the Federal Reserve System
www.federalreserve.gov

Bureau of Labor Statistics
www.bls.gov

Country Studies/Area Handbook (covers 92 countries)
lcweb2.loc.gov/frd/cs

The Economist Magazine
www.economist.com

FedStats: One Stop Shopping for Federal Statistics
www.fedstats.gov

Fifty States and Capitals
www.50states.com

Findlaw (directory of free legal and government resources)
www.findlaw.com

Foreign Government Resources on the Web
www.lib.umich.edu/govdocs/foreign.html

Gallup Opinion Polls
www.gallup.com

GPO (U.S. Government Printing Office)
www.gpoaccess.gov

The History Channel
www.thehistorychannel.com

InfoNation (information on 185 U.N. member countries)
cyberschoolbus.un.org/information3/menu/advanced.asp

IRS (tax publications and forms)
www.irs.gov

Library of Congress
www.loc.gov

Meta-Index for U.S. Legal Research
gsulaw.gsu.edu/metaindex

NASA
www.nasa.gov

NOLO: Law for All
www.nolo.com

Occupational Outlook Handbook
www.bls.gov/oco

OCLCPAIS (Public Affairs Information Service)
www.pais.org

POTUS: Presidents of the U.S.
www.ipl.org/div/potus

Thomas—U.S. Congress on the Internet
thomas.loc.gov

U.S. Copyright Office
www.copyright.gov

U.S. Postal Service
www.usps.com

**University of Michigan
    Document Center**
www.lib.umich.edu/govdocs

World Fact Book (information produced by
    the CIA on 267 countries)
www.cia.gov/cia/publications/factbook

Zip Code Look-Up
www.usps.gov/zip4

Humanities and Writing English Resources

Best of the Humanities on the Web
www.edsitement.neh.gov

Dictionary.com Writing Resources
dictionary.reference.com/writing

Guide to Writing Research Papers
www.ccc.commnet.edu/mla/index.shtml

Humanities Resources for Research
    (British Library)
www.bl.uk/collections/wider/
    humanities.html

Humbul Humanities Hub
www.humbul.ac.uk

Online Resources for Writers
webster.commnet.edu/writing/
    writing.htm

Open Directory Writers Resources
www.dmoz.org/Arts/Writers_Resources

Purdue University's Online Writing Lab
owl.english.purdue.edu

**Resources for Writers and Writing
    Instructors**
www.andromeda.rutgers.edu/~jlynch/
    Writing/links.html

Teacher Humanities Resources
www.minnesotahumanities.org/Teachers/
    resources.htm

Writing for the Web
www.useit.com/papers/webwriting

Writing on the Internet
www.webreference.com/internet/writing

Maps

Ersys
www.ersys.com

MapQuest
www.mapquest.com

National Geographic Map Machine
plasma.nationalgeographic.com/
    mapmachine

Perry-Castaneda Library Map Collection
    (2100 maps, not local maps)
www.lib.utexas.edu/maps

Topozone (topographical maps of the
    United States)
www.topozone.com

Museums

Computer History Museum
www.computer-history.org

Exploratorium (science museum)
www.exploratorium.edu

IEEE Virtual Museum
www.ieee-virtual-museum.org

Louvre
www.louvre.fr

The Metropolitan Museum of Art in NY
www.metmuseum.org

Museum of Modern Art, NYC
www.moma.org

National Gallery of Art
www.nga.gov

Open ALL Hours (UK Museums)
www.24hourmuseum.org.uk

The Smithsonian
www.si.edu

News Sources

ABC
www.abcnews.com

Associated Press
www.ap.org

BBC News
news.bbc.co.uk

CNN (Cable News Network)
www.cnn.com

CBS
www.cbs.com

CNET
www.news.com

ESPN (sports news)
www.espn.go.com

News Voyager
www.newspaperlinks.com

Internet News
www.internetnews.com

Internet Week
www.internetweek.com

Newsforge
www.newsforge.com

The New York Times
www.nytimes.com

Reuters
www.reuters.com

BIBLIOGRAPHY FOR FURTHER READING

Anderson, Rebecca S., Bauer, John F., & Speck, Bruce W. (Eds.). (2002). *Assessment strategies for the on-line class: From theory to practice.* San Francisco: Jossey-Bass.

Bare bones 101: A basic tutorial on searching the web. (2004, September 27). Retrieved December 2, 2004, from www.sc.edu/beaufort/library/pages/bones/bones.shtml

Berinstein, Paula. (2003). *Business statistics on the Web: Find them fast—at little or no cost.* Medford, NJ: CyberAge Books.

Berkman, Robert I. (2000). *Find it fast: How to uncover expert information on any subject online or in print.* New York: HarperResource.

Borrowman, S. (1999, spring). Critical surfing: Holocaust denial and credibility on the Web. *College Teaching, 47:2* [online] 6pp. Retrieved February 10, 2004 from: EBSCOhost Academic Search Elite.

Burkhardt, Joanna M., MacDonald, Mary C., & Rathemacher, Andrée J. (2003). *Teaching information literacy: 35 practical, standards-based exercises for college students.* Chicago: American Library Association.

Cannon, C. M. (2001, April). The real computer virus. *American Journalism Review, 23*(3), 28–35.

Calishain, Tara, Dornfest, Rael, & Adams, D. J. (2003). *Google pocket guide.* Sebastopol, CA: O'Reilly Media.

Chamberlain, Ellen. (2002). *Evaluating Website content.* Bloomington, IN: Phi Delta Kappa Educational Foundation.

Diaz, Karen R., & O'Hanlon, Nancy. (2004). *IssueWeb: A guide and sourcebook for researching controversial issues on the Web.* Westport, CT: Libraries Unlimited.

Duffy, M. E. (2003). Web of hate: A fantasy theme analysis of the rhetorical vision of hate groups online. *Journal of Communication Inquiry 27*(3), 291–312.

Edmonds, Graham. (2004). *The good Web site guide 2005.* Hammersmith, London: HarperCollins Publishers.

Fitzgerald, M. A. (1997). Misinformation on the Internet: Applying evaluation skills to online information. *Emergency Librarian, 24:3* [Online]. Retrieved February 14, 2004 from: Professional Development Collection Database, Number: 0315888.

Garvin, Peggy (Ed.). (2003). *Government information on the Internet* (6th ed.). Lanham, MD: Bernan Press.

Garvin, Peggy (Ed.). (2004). *The United States government Internet manual 2003–2004.* Lanham, MD: Bernan Press.

Glossbrenner, Alfred, & Glossbrenner, Emily. (2004). *Google and other search engines.* Berkeley, CA: Peachpit Press.

The good, the bad & the ugly: Why it's a good idea to evaluate Web sources. (2004, October 3). Retrieved December 2, 2004, from lib.nmsu.edu/instruction/eval.html

Gralla, Preston. (2004). *How the Internet works* (7th ed.). Indianapolis, IN: Que.

Hara, N., & Estrada, Z. (2003). Hate and peach in a connected world: Comparing MoveOn and Stromfront. *First Monday, 8:12* [Online], 25pp. Retrieved February 13, 2004 from: www.firstmonday.org. (February 13, 2004).

Hartman, Karen, & Ackermann, Ernest C. (2004). *Searching and researching on the Internet and the World Wide Web* (4th ed.). Wilsonville, OR: Franklin, Beedle, & Associates.

Henninger, Maureen. (2003). *The hidden Web: Finding quality information on the net.* Sydney, Australia: UNSW Press.

Hernon, Peter, Dugan, Robert E., & Shuler, John A. (2003). *U.S. government on the Web: Getting the information you need* (3rd ed.). Westport, CT: Libraries Unlimited.

Hill, Brad. (2003). *Google for dummies.* Indianapolis, IN: Wiley Publishing.

Hock, Randolph. (2004). *The extreme searcher's Internet handbook: A guide for the serious searcher.* Medford, NJ: CyberAge Books.

Kaye, Barbara K. (in press). It's a blog, blog, blog, blog world: Users and uses of weblogs. *Atlantic Journal of Communication, 13*(2).

Lee, E. & Leets, L. (2002, February). Persuasive storytelling by hate groups online. *American Behavioral Scientist, 45*(6), 923–957.

Leets, L. (2001). Responses to Internet hate sites: Is speech too free in cyberspace? *Communication Law & Policy, 6*(2), 287–318.

Levine, John R., Young, Margaret Levine, & Baroudi, Carol. (2003). *The Internet for dummies* (9th ed.). Hoboken, NJ: Wiley Publishing.

Milstein, Sarah, & Dornfest, Rael. (2004). *Google: The missing manual.* Sebastopol, CA: O'Reilly Media.

Mintz, Anne P. (Ed.). (2002). *Web of deception: Misinformation on the Internet.* Medford, NJ: CyberAge Books.

Pomeroy, Andrew M. (2002). *The research book: Mastering search engines.* Placentia, CA: Creative Continuum.

Recent and forthcoming Internet publications, 2004–2005. (2004). *Choice, 41*(Suppl.), 57–62.

RUSA Machine-Assisted Reference Section (MARS). (2004, Fall). Best free reference Web sites sixth annual list. *Reference & User Services Quarterly, 44*(1), 39–45. Retrieved March 6, 2005, from www.ala.org/ala/rusa/rusaourassoc/rusasections/mars/marspubs/MARSBestRef2004.htm

Schlein, Alan M. (2004). *Find it online: The complete guide to online research* (4th ed.). Tempe, AZ: Facts on Demand Press.

Tensen, Bonnie L. (2004). *Research strategies for a digital age.* Boston: Thomson Wadsworth.

Tomaiuolo, Nicholas G. (2004). *The Web library: Building a world class personal library with free Web resources.* Medford, NJ: CyberAge Books.

Williams, Jeremy B., & Jacobs, Joanne. (2004). Exploring the use of blogs as learning spaces in the higher education sector. *Australasian Journal of Education Technology, 20*(2), 232–247.

CHAPTER 2

Search Engines, Subject Directories, and Virtual Libraries

Your professor has just assigned you to give a five-minute speech on the topic of gun control. After a (hopefully brief) panic attack, you begin to think of what type of information you need to write the speech. To create an interesting introduction, you decide to involve your classmates by taking a straw poll of their views for and against gun control; next following this up by giving some statistics on how many people in the United States favor (or oppose) gun control legislation; and finally by outlining the arguments on both sides of the issue.

If you already know the correct URL for an authoritative website such as Gallup Opinion Polls (www.gallup.com) or other sites from Chapter 1, you are in great shape! However, what do you do when you don't have a clue as to which website has information on your topic? In these cases, many, many people routinely (and mistakenly) go to Google and type in a single term (e.g., *guns*). This approach is sure to bring first a smile to your face when the results offer you 200,874 hits on your topic, but just as quickly make you grind your teeth in frustration when you start scrolling down the hit list and find sites that range from gun dealerships, to reviews of the video *Young Guns,* to aging fan sites for Guns N' Roses.

Finding information on a specific topic on the Web is a challenge. The more intricate your research need, the more difficult it is to find the one or two best websites that feature the quality information you want. This chapter is designed to help you avoid frustration and focus in on the right site for your research by using search engines, subject directories, metasites, and virtual libraries.

SEARCH ENGINES

Search engines (sometimes called search services) have become more numerous on the Web (see Figures 2.1 and 2.2). Originally, they were designed to help users search the Web by topic. More recently, search engines have added features that enhance their usefulness, such as searching specific material on the Web (e.g., only sites of educational institutions—.edu), retrieving just one site that the search engine touts as most relevant (e.g., Ask Jeeves,

FIGURE 2.1 Google is one of the most popular search engines on the internet.
Reproduced with permission from Google, Inc. (www.google.com).

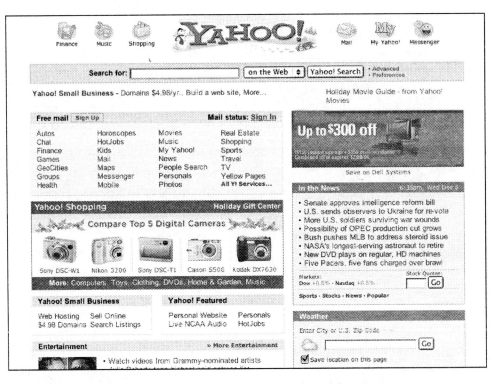

FIGURE 2.2   Yahoo! is also a very popular search engine on the Internet.

Reproduced with permission of Yahoo! Inc. © 2004 by Yahoo! Inc. Yahoo! and the Yahoo! logo are trademarks of Yahoo! Inc. (www.yahoo.com).

at www.aj.com), or retrieving up to 10 sites that the search engine ranks as most relevant (e.g., Google, at www.google.com).

According to Sullivan (2004), "Crawler-based search engines, such as Google, create their listings automatically. They 'crawl' or 'spider' the web, then people search through what they have found." Human-powered directories (like the Open Directory Project, www.dmoz.org) depend on human indexers to catalog their listings. Some search engines are hybrids (like MSN Search, search.msn.com) that use both crawler-based search engines and human indexers for their listings. Sullivan (2004) notes that there are three elements of a search engine:

1. Spider or Crawler—visits a web page, reads it, and follow links to other pages.
2. Index or Catalog—a copy of every web page that the spider finds.
3. Search Engine software—the program that uses a set of rules to match search queries to the index and to rank them in order of relevance.

One problem students often have in their use of search engines is that they are deceptively easy to use, like our search example of guns, no matter what is typed into the handy box at the top, links to numerous websites appear instantaneously, lulling students into a false sense of security. If so much was retrieved, surely *some* of it must be useful. *Wrong!* Many websites are very light on substantive content, which is not what you need for academic endeavors. Finding just the right website has been likened to finding diamonds in the desert.

As you can see by Sullivan's definition, one reason for this is that most search engines use indexes developed by machines. Therefore they are indexing terms not concepts. The search engine cannot tell the difference between the keyword *crack* meaning a split in the sidewalk, and *crack* referring to the street drug crack cocaine.

Google—The Search Engine Phenomenon

"To Google" has become a commonly used verb, which is perhaps the best indication of the search engine's astonishing popularity. "Google searches average 250 million searches per day, and the total daily number of Web searches is estimated at well over 600 million" (Vine, 2004a, p. 25). Indeed, four out of every five web searches use Google technology either at Google itself, or at its licensees like AOL and Yahoo! (Levy 2004).

The popularity of Google has largely come about because of its powerful and complex search algorithms (rules for searching and ranking) that allow searchers to get highly relevant results. These algorithms include PageRank™ that sorts results by the number of sites that link to a page thereby banking on the probability that a popular page will be useful. In addition, "Google remains the only search engine that still keeps paid results out of its main listings" (Vine 2004a, p. 26). This lack of commercialization has proved to be a major plus for users of Google, although since Google has gone public, there are questions as to how long this purity will remain since search engines get their profitability from their advertising.

The entrance of MSN Search (search.msn.com), and the updating of Yahoo!'s search algorithms will have a major impact on the competitive search engine market. One impact on serious searchers will be that they will have to understand that there will never be just one search engine for every need. "The increasing commercialization of search will require all serious searchers to have a 'search toolbox'—a list of start sites that they can return to when they don't already know the best starting points for their information search" (Vine 2004a, p. 30). (See Chapter 1, pp. 22–25 and Table 2.1 for a well stocked "search toolbox").

Vivisimo (www.vivisimo.com) has launched Clusty (www.clusty.com), which returns results in clusters by subcategory. It can be very helpful when searching broad subjects. Other search engines that provide results in clusters are Turbo10 (www.turbo10.com) and Wisenut (www.wisenut.com). KartOO (www.kartoo.com) returns results in interactive maps that visually represent connections between results.

"You know, tracking search engine news and updates can be a challenge. How to keep up? These sites will help you stay current:

- Search Engine Showdown (www.searchengineshowdown.com)
- Search Engine Watch (www.searchenginewatch.com)

Google obsessed? There is also a site devoted to tracking Google's moves:

- Watching Google Like a Hawk (www.wglah.com)

(From Vine, 2004b)

TABLE 2.1   Types of Search Engines

TYPE	DESCRIPTION	EXAMPLES
Crawler-Based Search Engines	Nonevaluative; does not evaluate results in terms of content or authority Results ordered by characteristics such as concept, document type, website, and popularity, rather than relevancy	**About.Com** www.about.com **AllTheWeb.com** www.alltheweb.com **AltaVista** www.altavista.com **Ask Jeeves** www.aj.com

••
TABLE 2.1   (continued)
••

TYPE	DESCRIPTION	EXAMPLES
		Direct Hit (Teoma) www.directhit.com **Excite** www.excite.com **Gigablast** www.gigablast.com **Google** www.google.com **Lycos** www.lycos.com **MSN Search** search.msn.com **Simplifind** www.simpli.com **Teoma** www.teoma.com
Directories/Portals	Provide additional features such as customized news, stock quotations, weather reports, shopping, and so forth Meant to be used as a one-stop web guide Profit from prominent advertisements and fees charged to featured sites Primarily compiled by human indexers	**GoGuides.org** www.GoGuides.org **Google Web Directory** directory.google.com **JoeAnt** www.JoeAnt.com **LookSmart** www.looksmart.com **My Starting Point** www.stpt.com **NBCi** www.nbci.com **Open Directory Project** www.dmoz.org **Skaffe.com** www.skaffe.com **Yahoo!** www.yahoo.com **Zeal** www.zeal.com

(continued)

• •

TABLE 2.1   (continued)

• •

TYPE	DESCRIPTION	EXAMPLES
Meta–search engines	Comprehensive search Display results for search engines in one rank-ordered list Remove duplicates Return only portions of results from each engine Allow you to choose which combination of search engines you want to search	**Beaucoup.com** www.beaucoup.com **Clusty** www.clusty.com **Dogpile** www.dogpile.com **GoHip** www.gohip.com **HotBot** www.HotBot.com **Icerocket** www.icerocket.com **KartOO** www.kartoo.com **Mamma** www.mamma.com **MetaCrawler** www.metacrawler.com **ProFusion** www.profusion.com **Surfwax** www.surfwax.com **Turbo10** www.turbo10.com **Veoda** www.veoda.com **Vivisimo** www.vivisimo.com **Wisenut** www.wisenut.com

QUICK TIPS FOR MORE EFFECTIVE USE OF SEARCH ENGINES

1. Use a search engine when
   - You have a narrow topic to search.
   - You want to search the full text of countless web pages.

- You want to retrieve a large number of sites.
- The features of the search engine (e.g., searching specific information on the Web) help with your search.
- You are searching a complex topic with more than one concept or subject (e.g., the effect of television violence on children).
- You want to use advanced search options.
- You want to search for a phrase or series of words (e.g., "total solar eclipse").

2. Always use Boolean operators to combine terms. Searching a single term is a sure way to retrieve a very large number of web pages, few, if any, of which are on target.

   - Always check the search engine Help feature to find what symbols are used for the operators as these vary (e.g., some engines use the & or + symbol for *AND*).

   - Boolean operators include the words *AND*—or use the plus sign (+) to narrow the search and to make sure that *both* terms are included (e.g., children *AND* violence); *OR*—to broaden the search and to make sure that *either* term is included (e.g., child *OR* children *OR* juveniles); and *NOT*—or use the minus sign (–) to *exclude* one term (e.g., eclipse *NOT* lunar).

   - When using the Boolean operator *OR*, try to think of as many terms as possible that suit your topic (e.g., solar *OR* sun *OR* lunar *OR* moon *AND* eclipse) rather than just solar *AND* eclipse. This will improve your search results.

3. Use appropriate symbols to indicate important terms and to indicate phrases (see the Tip on page 36).

4. Use word stemming (i.e., truncation) to find all variations of a word. (Check the search engine Help for symbols.)

   - If you want to retrieve *child, child's,* or *children*, use *child**. (Some engines use other symbols, such as !, #, or $.)

   - Some engines automatically search singular and plural terms. (Check Help to see whether yours does.)

5. Because search engines only search a portion of the Web, use several search engines or a meta–search engine to extend your reach.

6. Remember, search engines are mostly mindless drones that do not evaluate. Do not rely on them to find the best websites on your topic. Use subject directories or metasites to ensure value (see Table 2.2).

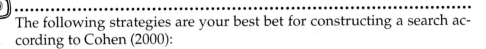

The following strategies are your best bet for constructing a search according to Cohen (2000):

> Use a plus sign (+) in front of terms you want to retrieve:
> +solar   +eclipse
>
> Place a phrase in double quotation marks: "solar eclipse"
>
> Combine the phrases   "+solar eclipse"   "+South America"

FINDING THOSE DIAMONDS IN THE DESERT: USING SUBJECT DIRECTORIES AND METASITES

Although search engines use algorithms to try to find the most relevant results, they do not make any judgment on the worth of the content. They just return a long, sometimes very long, list of sites that contained your keyword. However, human indexers, usually librarians or subject experts, have developed **subject directories,** which are defined by Cohen (1999) as follows:

> A subject directory is a service that offers a collection of links to Internet resources submitted by site creators or evaluators and organized into subject categories. Directory services use selection criteria for choosing links to include, though the selectivity varies among services. (p. 27)

Web subject directories are useful when you want to explore sites on your topic that have been reviewed, evaluated, and selected for their authority, accuracy, and value. (See Chapter 3 for an in-depth discussion of evaluation criteria.) They can be real time-savers for students because subject directories weed out the commercial, lightweight, or biased websites. Choose subject directories to ensure you are searching the highest-quality web pages. As an added bonus, subject directories periodically check weblinks to ensure fewer dead-end and out-dated links.

Metasites are similar to subject directories, but are more specific in nature, usually dealing with one scholarly field or discipline. Some examples of subject directories and metasites are found in Table 2.2 (see Figures 2.2 and 2.3 on pages 30 and 41).

TABLE 2.2   Smart Searching: Subject Directories, Metasites, and Portals

TYPE	EXAMPLES
General (covers many topics)	**About.com** www.about.com **Federal Web Locator** www.infoctr.edu/fwl **Galaxy** www.galaxy.com **Ibiblio: The Public's Library and Digital Archive** www.ibiblio.org **Infomine: Scholarly Internet Resource Collections** infomine.ucr.edu **InfoSurf: Help by Subject** www.library.ucsb.edu/subjects **Librarian's Index to the Internet** www.lii.org **Martindale's "The Reference Desk"** www.martindalecenter.com **Needle in a Cyberstack, the InfoFinder** www.home.mchsi.com/~albeej **PINAKES: A Subject Launchpad** www.hw.ac.uk/libWWW/irn/pinakes/pinakes.html **Refdesk** www.refdesk.com **Resource Shelf** www.resourceshelf.com **Selected Reference Sites** www.mnsfld.edu/depts/lib/mu-ref.html **Sparknotes** (online study guides) www.sparknotes.com **University of Delaware Library Subject Guides** www2.lib.udel.edu/subj **WWW Virtual Library** www.vlib.org
Subject Oriented Communication Studies	**First Monday** (online journal) www.firstmonday.org **Journal of Computer-Mediated Communication** jcmc.indiana.edu

(continued)

●●

TABLE 2.2 **(continued)**

●●

TYPE	EXAMPLES
Subject Oriented (*continued*) Communication Studies (*continued*)	**The Media and Communication Studies Site** www.aber.ac.uk/media/functions/mcs.html **North American Data Communications Museum** www.nadcomm.com **University of Iowa Department of Communication Studies** www.uiowa.edu/~commstud/resources
Cultural Studies	**Resource Center for Cyberculture Studies** www.com.washington.edu/rccs **Sarah Zupko's Cultural Studies Center** www.popcultures.com
Education	**Educational Virtual Library** www.csu.edu.au/education/library.html **GEM: The Gateway to Educational Materials** (US Dept. of Education) www.thegateway.org **Kathy Schrock's Guide for Educators** school.discovery.com/schrockguide **Math Forum** (for math educators) www.mathforum.org
English and Humanities	**Best of the Humanities on the Web** www.edsitement.neh.gov **Dictionary.com Writing Resources** dictionary.reference.com/writing **Guide to Writing Research Papers** www.ccc.commnet.edu/mla/index.shtml **Humanities Resources for Research (British Library)** www.bl.uk/collections/wider/humanities.html **Humbul Humanities Hub** www.humbul.ac.uk **Open Directory Writer's Resources** www.dmoz.org/Arts/Writers_Resources **Online Resoruces for Writers** www.webster.comment.edu/writing/writing.htm **Purdue University's Online Writing Lab** owl.english.purdue.edu

TABLE 2.2   (continued)

TYPE	EXAMPLES
Subject Oriented *(continued)* English and Humanities *(continued)*	**Resources for Writers and Writing Instructors** www.andromeda.rutgers.edu/~jlynch/Writing/links.html **Teacher Humanities Resources** www.minnesotahumanities.org/Teachers/resources.htm **Writing for the Web** www.webreference.com/internet/writing **Writing on the Internet** www.webreference.com/internet/writing
Journalism	**Journalism Resources** bailiwick.lib.uiowa.edu/journalism **Thinkquest** library.thinkquest.org/library
Literature	**A Celebration of Women Writers** www.digital.library.upenn.edu/women **Literary Criticism** (Internet Public Library) www.ipl.org/ref/litcrit **Norton Anthology of American Literature** www.wwnorton.com/naal **Project Gutenberg** (over 12,000 full text titles) www.gutenberg.org **World Wide Words** (History of English language and new word development) www.worldwidewords.org
E-books	**Alex Catalogue of Electronic Texts** www.infomotions.com/alex **Amazon Ebooks & Documents** www.amazon.com/exec/obidos/tg/browse/-/551440 **Badosa** www.badosa.com **Banned Books Online** www.digital.library.upenn.edu/books/banned-books.html **Bartleby.com** www.bartleby.com

(continued)

TABLE 2.2   (continued)

TYPE	EXAMPLES
Subject Oriented *(continued)* E-books *(continued)*	**Bibliomania** www.bibliomania.com **Digital Content for Adobe Reader** bookstore.glassbook.com/store/default.asp **Electronic Text Center** etext.virginia.edu/ebooks **EServer.org: Accessible Writing** www.eserver.org **Free ebooks.net** www.free-ebooks.net **Humanities Text Initiative** www.hti.umich.edu **Internet Classics Archive** (440+ free classics) classics.mit.edu/index.html **NetLibrary** www.netlibrary.com **The Online Books Page** onlinebooks.library.upenn.edu **Perseus Digital Library** www.perseus.tufts.edu **Project Gutenberg** www.gutenberg.org
Medicine & health	**Go Ask Alice** (health and sexuality) www.goaskalice.columbia.edu **Medline Plus** www.medlineplus.com **PubMed** (National Library of Medicine's index to medical journals, 1966 to present) www.pubmed.gov **RxList: The Internet Drug Index** www.rxlist.com **WebMD** www.webmd.com **Where to Find MSDS (Materials Safety Data Sheets) on the Internet** www.ilpi.com/msds

··

TABLE 2.2   (continued)

··

TYPE	EXAMPLES

Subject Oriented
(continued)

Science & Technology

CNET
www.cnet.com

Earthtrends: The Environmental Information Portal
www.earthtrends.wri.org

**Eric Weisstein's World of Science: A Wolfram
  Web Resource**
scienceworld.wolfram.com

NIST Chemistry Web Book
webbook.nist.gov/chemistry

Pew Internet and American Life
www.pewinternet.org

Plants Database
plants.usda.gov

SciCentral
www.scicentral.com

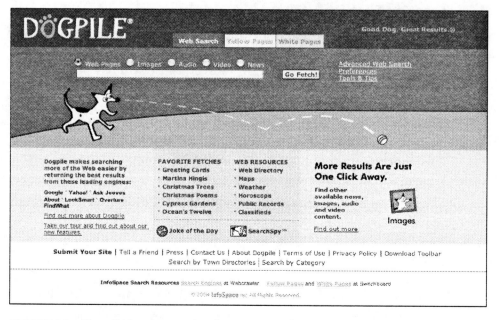

FIGURE 2.3   Dogpile is an example of a meta–search engine (www.dogpile.com).

VIRTUAL LIBRARIES AND ASK-A-LIBRARIAN SERVICES

Virtual Libraries

Another closely related group of sites that are a valuable and usually underutilized resource for college students is their *virtual library* site, sometimes called *digital library* site. With few exceptions, every college library has a home page for easy on-campus and off-campus access to an array of electronic resources. Most library websites provide links to free web-based websites and also to fee-based subscriptions that are only accessible to students and faculty of their particular university. These sites are useful, because, like subject directories and metasites, information professionals have organized websites by topic and selected only those of highest quality. Unfortunately, many students are unaware of these sites and miss out on very useful and highly authoritative resources selected by their university librarians.

"Why Use the Library Instead of Google? Or Yahoo!, or AltaVista . . . "

An article with this name by Brian Simpson appeared in the Johns Hopkins University magazine in February 2003. It listed four reasons to use library resources delivered through the web rather than searching on your own. These are summarized here:

- **Time** (You can save lots by using virtual or print library collections, or asking a librarian.)
- **Money** (You are paying for many of these services with your tuition dollars—makes sense to use them!)
- **Disgrace** (Avoid the embarrassment of citing inappropriate sources in your papers.)
- **Sanity** (Information in the library is well organized and easily accessible, the Web is not.)

At the Johns Hopkins University Library, their slogan is "Ask a librarian . . . the ultimate search engine."

Ask-A-Librarian Services— Help at Your Computer!

Can't get to the library? Working from home and need some information that you can't find on Google or MSN Search? Getting frustrated or feeling lost? Did you know that an increasing number of university library home pages are now offering live or email "Ask-A-Librarian" services for free? These services have come into being to provide students with librarian help at their desktop instead of needing to come into the library building.

Did you also know that Craig Silverstein, Google's Director of Technology, has said that search engines are still "hundreds of years away" from being "as smart as a reference librarian" according to the *Library Journal Academic News Wire*, May 13, 2003. Check your campus library's web page, or call the reference desk to find out if your library offers a chat or email reference service.

For example, in 2001, Wallace Library at the Rochester Institute of Technology (RIT) started live chat sessions with their librarians who were assigned to handle different Colleges within the Institute. This service was especially helpful for students attending RIT's National Technical Institute for the Deaf (NTID) and RIT's large number of distance education students. Presently, over 400 students a year participate in this interactive service. (See Figure 2.4.)

In addition, because so many new college students are Internet savvy, in September 2004, RIT introduced a new Instant Messaging (IM) library service called "One-2-One Live Reference Help." (See Figure 2.5.) IM is available during the day until 10 P.M. for currently enrolled RIT students to contact a librarian live at the reference desk. During the first month of service, librarians received over 100 instant messages and the NTID librarians averaged 15 per week. One can only image how this number has increased as students learned about the IM service. As technologies change, so do the ways in which librarians interact with students!

If you have found that your college does not have an Ask-A-Librarian service, check your local public library's web page. Several states (e.g., Massachusetts, New Jersey, Florida, Washington, and Maryland) now have

FIGURE 2.4 The Wallace Library site at the Rochester Institute of Technology (RIT) is an outstanding example of a virtual library on the Internet.

Reprinted with permission from Wallace Library, Rochester Institute of Technology (wally.rit.edu).

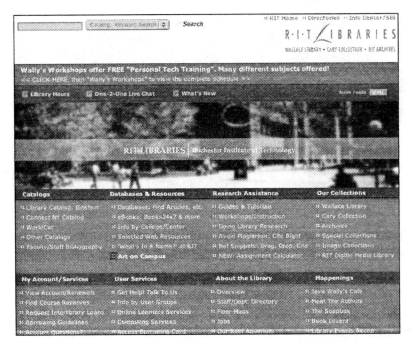

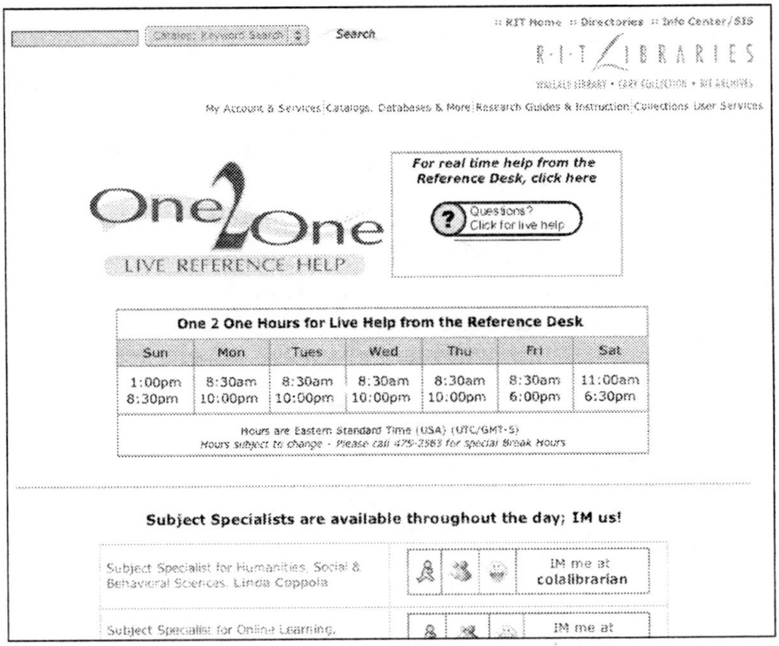

FIGURE 2.5 One-2-One IM Service at the Wallace Library at RIT.

Reprinted with permission from Wallace Library, Rochester Institute of Technology (wally.rit.edu).

statewide "Ask-A-Librarian" services, which are easily accessible through the Web. Some of these services have limited hours and some are available 24 hours a day, 365 days a year. Check your library's website for details. If all else fails, you can email the Library of Congress at www.loc.gov (see Figure 2.6), but you will not get an instant reply. To get you started, these recommendations will save you time and help you to get the most from using an "Ask-A-Librarian" chat reference.

Recommendations for Using Ask-A-Librarian Chat Virtual Reference Services

BEFORE YOU SIGN ON

- Don't wait until the last minute before using a chat reference service. These services are becoming busier. Just like your experiences at a regular library reference or information desk, there may be a queue of users ahead of you.

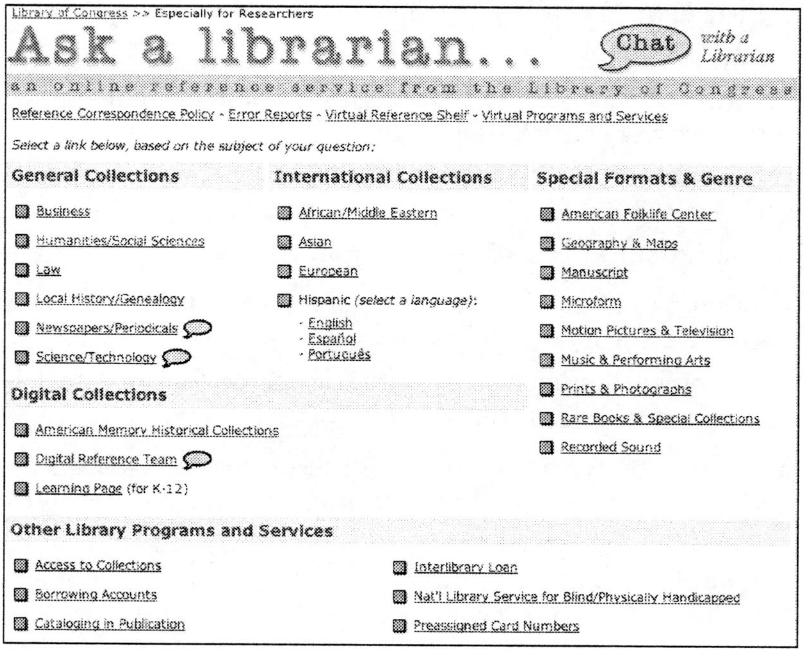

FIGURE 2.6 Even the Library of Congress has an Ask-A-Librarian Service, which is both email- and chat-based. Professional librarians are available to answer your research questions.

Reprinted with permission from the Library of Congress (www.loc.gov).

- Don't expect an immediate answer. Depending on how complex your query is, the librarian may take several minutes to search. If you are in a hurry, tell the librarian your time constraints when you sign on.

  Example: "I need information on the impact of TV violence. I have to leave this computer station in 10 minutes, can you help me quickly?" (If the librarian can't, he/she will tell you.)

  Instead of: "Help me find information on TV violence. I am in a hurry!"

- Think about your topic. Write down your question in a short, specific statement that helps the librarian to focus on

  - Topic
  - Type of resources you need
  - Amount of information needed
  - Any additional information you think would help

    Example: "I need recent journal articles about the impact of TV violence on teens for a 10-page paper for my undergraduate communication class. It is due in seven days."

    Instead of: "I need information on TV violence."

- Write down a list of the resources you have already checked so far. The librarian may ask: "Have you checked the library's online catalog yet?" If you are just starting, tell the librarian.

  Example: "I need statistics on gun violence for a debate. I am just getting started and don't know where to begin."

  Instead of: "I need statistics on gun violence."

- If you have already located an ideal resource, tell the librarian. If you know of a title or author, give this information.

  Example: "I found a great journal article on this topic by J. Doe, published in the *Atlantic Monthly*."

- Think of synonyms and alternative terms for the topic, both narrower and broader. The librarian may ask you for other subject terms.

  Example: Term is "teen." Alternative terms are "adolescent, young adult, teenager, or juvenile." Narrower: "boyhood, or girl;" Broader: "young person, youth, or minor."

DURING THE CHAT SESSION
- Use short replies and hit the send button between sentences.
- Be informal, but courteous. Use polite expressions as appropriate. Acknowledge humor.

- Don't be afraid to admit you don't know something or have just begun to look for information. It is okay to say "I don't know" or "I'm not sure" or even "I am confused."

- Give feedback when asked. The librarian is trying to understand your question with probe questions.

- Be patient! Expect some "delayed reactions" from the librarian. Remember that some questions require searching several websites.

- Be persistent. If you have a multi-part question, tell the librarian at the beginning and remind him/her gently before ending the session.

ENDING THE CHAT SESSION

- If you have to disconnect or leave the computer suddenly, tell the librarian, and indicate how long you will be gone.

  Example: Use "BRB" (be right back) or "Got to go! Will sign back on in 10 mins." Or "I have to go now. Please email me the information (and give your email address if necessary)."

- Ask the librarian to email you the transcript of the session at the end. This is frequently possible and useful for later reference.

- When you want to end, tell the librarian. A "thank-you" and closing statement are always appreciated and signal the librarian that you are ending the session.

  Example: "I have to go now, thanks so much for your help, good-bye."

Here are some examples of Ask-A-Librarian Services:

Florida Ask-A-Librarian	www.askalibrarian.org
Library of Congress Ask-A-Librarian	www.loc.gov/rr/askalib (see Figure 2.6)
Maryland AskUsNow!	www.askusnow.info
Massachusetts MassAnswers	www.massanswers.org
New Jersey Q and A	www.qandanj.org

Hopefully your college library has an outstanding website for both on and off-campus access to digital resources and an Ask-A-Librarian email or chat service. If not, you can access several virtual library sites that are listed in Table 2.3, although some of the resources may be subscription based (usually journal indexes like *Academic Search Premier*, or *Lexis-Nexis*, or high quality

∙∙

TABLE 2.3   Virtual Library Sites and Digital Image Collections

∙∙

Public Libraries

Internet Public Library	www.ipl.org
New York Public Library	www.nypl.org

University/College Libraries

Bucknell	www.bucknell.edu/isr
Case Western	www.cwru.edu/uclibraries.html
Dartmouth	diglib.dartmouth.edu
Duke	www.lib.duke.edu
Franklin and Marshall	www.library.fandm.edu
Harvard	lib.harvard.edu
Penn State	www.libraries.psu.edu
Princeton	www.princeton.edu/main/library
Rochester Institute of Technology	wally.rit.edu
Rutgers, The State University of New Jersey	www.libraries.rutgers.edu
Stanford	www.stanford.edu/home/libraries
Texas Lutheran University	bulldogs.tlu.edu
UCLA	www.library.ucla.edu
University of the Virgin Islands	library.uvi.edu
William Paterson University	www.wpunj.edu/library
Yale University	www.library.yale.edu

Special Library

Library of Congress	www.loc.gov

Digital Image Collections

American Memory	lcweb.loc.gov/ammem
NYPL Digital Gallery	digitalgallery.nypl.org/nypl digital
The NYPL Picture Collection	digital.nypl.org/mmpco
Picture History	www.picturehistory.com

subject databases like *Gale's Reference Shelf*) and accessible only to students of that particular university or college. These sites are useful because, like subject directories and metasites, experts have organized web resources by topic and selected only those of the highest quality.

SUMMARY
··················

In this chapter you read about

- Types of search engines
    Google—the phenomenon
    Crawler-based search engines
    Subject Directories/Metasites—offer a range of customized features
    Meta–search engines—search multiple search engines
- Virtual Libraries and Ask-A-Librarian services

You now know how to search for information and use search engines more effectively. In the next two chapters, you learn more tips for evaluating the information that you find and for citing it properly.

BIBLIOGRAPHY FOR FURTHER READING
··

Badke, William B. (2004). *Research strategies: Finding your way through the information fog* (2nd ed.). New York: iUniverse.

Barker, Donald I., & Terry, Carol D. (2005). *Internet research: Illustrated* (2nd ed.). Boston: Course Technology.

Best search engines quick guide. (2004, April 17). Retrieved December 6, 2004, from www.infopeople.org/search/guide.html

Best search tools chart. (2004, April 17). Retrieved December 6, 2004, from www .infopeople.org/search/chart.html

Bradley, Phil. (2002). *Internet power searching: The advanced manual* (2nd ed.). New York: Neal-Schuman.

Bradley, Phil. (2004). *The advanced Internet searcher's handbook* (3rd ed.). London: Facet.

Busby, Michael. (2004). *Learn Google.* Plano, TX: Wordware.

Calishain, Tara. (2004). *Web search garage.* Upper Saddle River, NJ: Prentice Hall.

Calishain, Tara, & Dornfest, Rael. (2003). *Google hacks: 100 industrial strength tips and tricks.* Sebastopol, CA: O'Reilly Media.

Cohen, Laura B. (2000, August). Searching the Web: The human element emerges. *CHOICE Supplement 37,* 17–31.

Cohen, Sharron. (2003). *The mysteries of Internet research.* Fort Atkinson, WI: Upstart-Books.

Cohen, Steven M. (2003). *Keeping current: Advanced Internet strategies to meet librarian and patron needs.* Chicago: American Library Association.

Finding information on the Internet: A tutorial. (2004, August 18). Retrieved December 6, 2004, from www.lib.berkeley.edu/TeachingLib/Guides/Internet/FindInfo.html

Friedman, Barbara. (2004). *Web search savvy: Strategies and shortcuts for online research.* Mahwah, NJ: Lawrence Erlbaum.

Internet navigation tools. (2003). Retrieved December 6, 2004, from www.rice.edu/Internet

Internet tutorials. (2004, October). Retrieved December 6, 2004, from library.albany.edu/internet

Levy, Steven. (2004, March 29). All eyes on Google. *Newsweek, 143*(13), 48–58.

McHugh, Josh. (2003, January). Google vs. evil. *Wired, 11*(1), 130–135.

Miller, Michael. (2003). *The complete idiot's guide to online search secrets.* Indianapolis, IN: Que.

O'Hara, Shelley. (2004). *Easy Google.* Indianapolis, IN: Que.

Schneider, Fritz, Blachman, Nancy, & Fredricksen, Eric. (2004). *How to do everything with Google.* Emeryville, CA: McGraw-Hill.

Stacey, Alison, & Stacey, Adrian. (2004). *Effective information retrieval from the Internet: An advanced user's guide.* Oxford, England: Chandos.

Sullivan, Danny. (2002, October 14). *How search engines work.* Retrieved December 6, 2004, from searchenginewatch.com/webmasters/article.php/2168031

Taylor, Paige & Lejeune, Jerri. (2004). *Consider the source: Finding reliable information on the internet.* Fort Atkinson, WI: UpstartBooks.

Tenopir, Carol. (2004, April 1). Is Google the competition? *Library Journal, 129*(6), 30.

Timesaver Books. (2003). *Google in 30 pages or less.* Champlain, NY: Timesaver Books.

Tool kit for the expert Web searcher. (2004, July 21). Retrieved December 6, 2004, from www.ala.org/ala/lita/litaresources/toolkitforexpert/toolkitexpert.htm

Vine, Rita. (2004, February). The business of search engines. *Information Outlook, 8*(2), 25–31.

Vine, Rita. (2004, March). Staying up to date in the ever-changing Web search world. *Information Outlook, 8*(3), 30–34.

Young, Jeffery R. (2004, December 3). Google has unveiled a search engine that focuses on scholarly materials, including peer-reviewed papers, theses, and technical reports. *The Chronicle of Higher Education, 51*(15), A34.

Zietman, Clive, & Zietman, Bettina. (2003). *The incredibly indispensable Web directory* (4th ed.). London: Kogan Page.

Content
Evaluation

Bingo! You've hit the jackpot! You've found a great website. Now what? The website you are viewing on your monitor seems like *the* perfect website for your research. But, are you sure? Why is it perfect? What criteria are you using to determine whether this website suits your purpose?

Think about it. Where on earth can anyone "publish" information regardless of the accuracy, currency, or reliability of the information? The Internet has opened up a world of opportunity for posting and distributing information and ideas to virtually everyone, even those who might post bogus information for fun, or those with ulterior motives for promoting their point of view. Armed with the guidelines provided in this chapter, you can dig through the vast amount of useless information on the World Wide Web to uncover the valuable information. Because practically anyone can post and distribute their ideas on the Web, you need to develop a new set of critical thinking skills that focus on the evaluation and quality of information, rather than be influenced and manipulated by slick graphics and flashy moving java scripts.

Way back before the existence of online sources, the validity and accuracy of a source was more easily determined. For example, when a book gets to the publishing stage, it has gone through many critiques, validation of facts, reviews, editorial changes, and so forth. Furthermore, ownership is clear because the author's name is attached to it. The publisher's reputation is on the line too. If the book turns out to have bogus information, reputations and money can be lost. In addition, books available in your university library are further reviewed by professional librarians and selected for library purchase because of their accuracy and value to students. Journal articles downloaded or printed from online subscription services, such as Infotrac, ProQuest, EBSCOhost, or other full-text databases, are put through the same scrutiny as the paper versions of the journals.

On the Web, however, Internet service providers (ISPs) simply give website authors a place to store information. The website author can post information that may not be validated or tested for accuracy. One mistake students typically make is to assume that all information on the Web is of equal value. Also, in the rush to get assignments in on time, students may not take the extra time to make sure that the information they are citing is accurate. It is easy to just cut and paste without really thinking about the content in a critical way. However, to make sure you are gathering accurate information and to get the best grade on your assignments, it is vital that you develop your critical ability to sift through the dirt to find those diamond nuggets.

WEB EVALUATION CRITERIA

So, here you are, at this potentially great site. Let's go through some ways you can determine if this site is one you can cite with confidence in your research. Keep in mind, ease of use is an issue, but learning how to determine the validity of data, facts, and statements is worthy of your time. The five traditional ways to check a paper source can also be applied to your web source: accuracy, authority, objectivity, coverage, and currency.

Accuracy

As described in Chapter 1, Internet searches are not the same as searches of library databases because much of the information on the Web has not been edited whereas information in databases has. It is your responsibility to make sure that the information you use in a school project is accurate. When you examine the content on a website or web page, you can ask yourself a number of questions to determine whether the information is accurate.

"When in doubt, leave the information out."

1. Is the information reliable?

2. Do the facts from your other research contradict the facts you find on this web page?

3. Do any misspellings and/or grammar mistakes indicate a hastily put-together website that has not been checked for accuracy?

4. Is the content on the page verifiable through some other source? Can you find similar facts elsewhere (journals, books, or other online sources) to support the facts you see on this web page?

5. Do you find links to other websites on a similar topic? If so, check those links to ascertain whether they back up the information you see on the web page you are interested in using.

6. Is a bibliography of additional sources for research provided? Lack of a bibliography doesn't mean the page isn't accurate, but having one allows you further investigation points to check the information.

7. Does the site of a research document or study explain how the data was collected and the type of research method used to interpret the data?

If you've found a site with information that seems too good to be true, it may be. You need to verify information that you read on the Web by cross-checking against other sources.

Authority

Important questions to ask when you are evaluating a website are: Who is the author of the information? Do you know whether the author is a recognized authority in his or her field? Biographical information, references to publications, degrees, qualifications, and organizational affiliations can help to indicate an author's authority. For example, if you are researching the topic of laser surgery, citing a medical doctor would be better than citing a college student who has had laser surgery.

The organization sponsoring the site can also provide clues about whether the information is fact or opinion. Examine how the information was gathered and the research method used to prepare the study or report. Other questions to ask include

1. Who is responsible for the content of the page? Although a webmaster's name is often listed, this person is not necessarily responsible for the content.
2. Is the author recognized in the subject area? Does this person cite any other publications he or she has authored?
3. Does the author list his or her background or credentials (e.g., Ph.D. degree, title such as professor, or other honorary or social distinction)?
4. Is there a way to contact the author? Does the author provide a phone number or email address?
5. If the page is mounted by an organization, is it a known, reputable one?
6. How long has the organization been in existence?
7. Does the URL for the web page end in the **extension** .edu or .org? Such extensions indicate authority, compared to dotcoms (.com), which are commercial enterprises. (For example, www.cancer.com takes you to an online drugstore that has a cancer information page; www.cancer.org is the American Cancer Society website.)

Ask yourself whether the author or organization presenting the information on the Web is an authority on the subject. If the answer is no, this may not be a good source of information.

Objectivity

Every author has a point of view, and some views are more controversial than others. Journalists try to be objective by providing both sides of a story. Academics attempt to persuade readers by presenting a logical argument, which cites other scholars' work. You need to look for two-sided arguments in news and information sites. For academic papers, you need to determine how the paper fits within its discipline and whether the author is using controversial methods for reporting a conclusion.

Authoritative authors situate their work within a larger discipline. This background helps readers evaluate the author's knowledge on a particular subject. You should ascertain whether the author's approach is controversial and whether he or she acknowledges this. More important, is the information being presented as fact or opinion? Authors who argue for their position provide readers with other sources that support their arguments. If no sources are cited, the material may be an opinion piece rather than an objective presentation of information. The following questions can help you determine objectivity:

1. Is the purpose of the site clearly stated, either by the author or the organization authoring the site?
2. Does the site give a balanced viewpoint or present only one side?
3. Is the information directed toward a specific group of viewers?
4. Does the site contain advertising?
5. Does the copyright belong to a person or an organization?
6. Do you see anything to indicate who is funding the site?

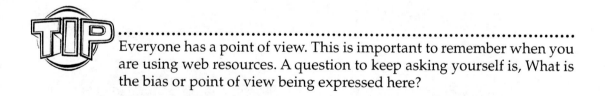

Everyone has a point of view. This is important to remember when you are using web resources. A question to keep asking yourself is, What is the bias or point of view being expressed here?

Coverage

Coverage deals with the breadth and depth of information presented on a website. Stated another way, it is about how much information is presented and how detailed the information is. Looking at the site map or index can give you an idea about how much information is contained on a site. This isn't necessarily bad. Coverage is a criteria that is tied closely to *your* research requirement. For one assignment, a given website may be too general for your needs. For another assignment, that same site might be perfect. Some sites contain very little actual information because pages are filled with links to other sites.

Coverage also relates to objectivity. You should ask the following questions about coverage:

"Don't be impressed by Web Page Awards. The joke going around the Web is, there are so many different awards that every web page has at least one."

1. Does the author present both sides of the story, or is a piece of the story missing?

2. Is the information comprehensive enough for your needs?

3. Does the site cover too much, too generally?

4. Do you need more specific information than the site can provide?

5. Does the site have an objective approach?

> **TIP**
>
> In addition to examining what is covered on a website, equally revealing is what is not covered. Missing information can reveal a bias in the material. Keep in mind that you are evaluating the information on a website for your research requirements.

Currency

Currency questions deal with the timeliness of information. However, currency is more important for some topics than for others. For example, currency is essential when you are looking for technology-related topics and current events. In contrast, currency may not be relevant when you are doing research on Plato or Ancient Greece. In terms of websites, currency also pertains to whether the site is being kept up to date and links are being maintained. Sites on the Web are sometimes abandoned by their owners. When people move or change jobs, they may neglect to remove their site from the company or university server. To test currency, ask the following questions:

1. Does the site indicate when the content was created?

2. Does the site contain a last revised date? How old is the date? (In the early part of 2001, a university website gave a last updated date of

1901! This date was obviously a Y2K problem, but it does point out the need to be observant of such things!)

3. Does the author state how often he or she revises the information? Some sites are on a monthly update cycle (e.g., a government statistics page).

4. Can you tell specifically what content was revised?

5. Is the information still useful for your topic? Even if the last update is old, the site might still be worthy of use *if* the content is still valid for your research.

RELEVANCY TO YOUR RESEARCH: PRIMARY VERSUS SECONDARY SOURCES

Some research assignments require the use of primary (original) sources. Materials such as raw data, diaries, letters, manuscripts, and original accounts of events can be considered primary material. In most cases, these historical documents are no longer copyrighted. The Web is a great source for this type of resource.

Information that has been analyzed and previously interpreted is considered a secondary source. Sometimes secondary sources are more appropriate than primary sources. If, for example, you are asked to analyze a topic or to find an analysis of a topic, a secondary source of an analysis would be most appropriate. Ask yourself the following questions to determine whether the website is relevant to your research:

1. Is it a primary or secondary source?

2. Do you need a primary source?

3. Does the assignment require you to cite different types of sources? For example, are you supposed to use at least one book, one journal article, and one web page?

HELP IN EVALUATING WEBSITES

As described in Chapter 1, one shortcut to finding high-quality websites is using subject directories and metasites, which select the websites they index by similar evaluation criteria to those just described. If you want to learn more about evaluating websites, many colleges and universities provide sites that help you evaluate web resources. The following list contains some excellent examples of these evaluation sites:

- Evaluating Quality on the Net—Hope Tillman, Babson College www.hopetillman.com/findqual.html
- Critical Web Evaluation—Kurt W. Wagner, William Paterson University of New Jersey   euphrates.wpunj.edu/faculty/wagnerk/critical.html
- Evaluating Web Sites: Criteria and Tools—Michael Engle, Cornell University   www.library.cornell.edu/olinuris/ref/research/webeval.html

A comparison of the criteria used by several noted web evaluation sites can be found in Table 3.1. Many books also contain information on web evaluation and on how the Web is being used unscrupulously. These books may point out what sites to stay away from. See the Bibliography for Further Reading at the end of Chapter 1 for a list of such books.

Using your common sense can also help you evaluate websites. For example, spelling mistakes and poor grammar indicate that a site has not been carefully checked for accuracy.

TABLE 3.1   Comparison of Web Evaluation Sites

WEBSITE AND URL	SOURCE	CRITERIA
Critical Thinking in an Online World www.library.ucsb.edu/ untangle/jones.html	University of California, Santa Barbara Library (Cabrillo College Internet librarian)	Fact vs. opinion, examine assumptions, be flexible and open-minded, be aware of ambiguity, look for reputable sources, focus on whole picture
Educom Review: Information Literacy as a Liberal Art www.educause.edu/pub/er/review/ reviewArticles/31231.html	EDUCAUSE (an organization focusing on information technology and education)	—
Evaluating Information Found on the Internet www.library.jhu.edu/research help/general/evaluating	Johns Hopkins University Library	Author, publishing body, academic credibility, currency

TABLE 3.1 (continued)

WEBSITE AND URL	SOURCE	CRITERIA
Evaluating Internet Information medlib.med.utah.edu/ed/ eduservices/infoeval.php	University of Utah Library	Author, publisher/sponsor, credibility bias/purpose, currency, site organization
Evaluating Web Sites www.lib.purdue.edu/rguides/ studentinstruction/evaluation/ evaluatingwebsites.html	Purdue University Library	Author, link to local home page, institution, date of evaluation creation/ revision, intended audience, purpose
Evaluating Web Resources www.delta.edu/library/ evaluating.html	Delta College (English teacher)	Author, publisher, credibility, agenda/purpose/bias, documentation, currency
Evaluating Web Resources www2.widener.edu/ Wolfram-Memorial-Library/ webevaluation/webeval.htm	Widener University Library	Accuracy, authority, objectivity, currency, coverage
Judging Quality on the Internet www.open.uoguelph.ca/ resources/skills/judging.html	University of Guelph Ontario, Canada	Generation of source, validity, credibility, audience and purpose, currency, bias, documentation
Kathy Schrock's ABC's of Web Site Evaluation www.kathyschrock.net/abceval	Author's website	Authorship, currency, spelling accuracy, credibility, relevance, bias, publisher
Resource Selection and Information Evaluation alexia.lis.uiuc.edu/~janicke/ Evaluate.html	University of Illinois, Urbana-Champaign (Illinois State University librarian)	Format, scope, relation to other works, authority, treatment, arrangement, cost
Testing the Surf: Criteria for Evaluating Internet Information Sources info.lib.uh.edu/pr/v8/n3/smit8n3.html	University of Houston	Accuracy, authority, currency, grammar, purpose and audience
UCLA College Library Instruction: Thinking Critically about World Wide Web Resources www.library.ucla.edu/libraries/ college/help/critical	UCLA Library	Audience, purpose, accuracy, author/producer, credibility, publisher, bias, graphical clarity
Web Evaluation: Criteria lib.nmsu.edu/instruction/evalcrit.html	New Mexico State University Library	Accuracy, author, bias/ objectivity, currency, coverage

SUMMARY

In this chapter you read about

- Evaluating websites using five criteria to judge website content:
    Accuracy—How reliable is the information?
    Authority—Who is the author and what are his or her credentials?
    Objectivity—Does the website present a balanced or biased point of view?
    Coverage—Is the information comprehensive enough for your needs?
    Currency—Is the website up to date?
- Using additional criteria to judge website content, including publisher, documentation, relevance, scope, audience, appropriateness of format, and navigation
- Judging whether the site is made up of primary (original) or secondary (interpretive) sources
- Determining whether the information is relevant to your research
- Where to go for additional help in evaluating websites
- The best evaluation websites and the criteria they use

CRITICAL EVALUATION WEBSITES

Critical Thinking in an Online World
www.library.ucsb.edu/untangle/jones.html

Critical Web Evaluation
euphrates.wpunj.edu/faculty/wagnerk/
    critical.html

Evaluation Criteria, Susan Beck
lib.nmsu.edu/instruction/evalcrit.html

**Evaluating Information Found
    on the Internet**
www.library.jhu.edu/researchhelp/general/
    evaluating

Judging Quality on the Net
www.open.uoguelph.ca/resources/skills/
    judging.html

**Kathy Schrock's the ABC's
    of Web Evaluation**
www.kathyschrock.net/abceval/

**Resource Selection and
    Information Evaluation**
alexia.lis.uiuc.edu/~janicke/Evaluate.html

Selecting the Right Source
www.library.ucla.edu/libraries/college/help/
    selectsource/

Ten C's for Evaluating Web Sites
www.uwec.edu/Library/Guides/tencs.html

**Testing the Surf: Criteria for Evaluating
    Internet Information Resources**
info.lib.uh.edu/pr/v8/n3/smit8n3.html

BIBLIOGRAPHY FOR FURTHER READING

Ackermann, Ernest C., & Hartman, Karen. (2004). *Searching and researching on the Internet & World Wide Web* (4th ed.). Wilsonville, OR: Franklin Beedle & Assoc.

Chamberlain, Ellen. (2002). *Evaluating website content.* Bloomington, Ind.: Phi Delta Kappa Educational Foundation.

Dragulanescu, Nicolae-George. (2002, September). Website quality evaluations: Criteria and tools. *International Information & Library Review, 34*(3), 247–255.

Hock, Randolph, & Price, Gary. (2004). *Extreme searcher's Internet handbook: A guide for the serious searcher.* Medford, N.J.: Cyberage Books.

Jacobson, Trudi. (2000). *Critical thinking and the Web: Teaching users to evaluate Internet resources.* Pittsburgh: Library Instruction Publications.

Ratner, Julie (2003). *Human factors and web development* (2nd ed.). Mahwah, N.J.: Lawrence Erlbaum Assoc.

Schlein, Alan M., Weber, Peter, & Newby, J. J. (2002). *Find it online: The complete guide to online research* (3rd ed.). Tempe, Ariz.: Facts on Demand Press.

Seoyoung Hong, & Jinwoo Kim. (2004, Sept/Oct). Architectural criteria for website evaluation—conceptual framework and empirical validation. *Behaviour & Information Technology, 23*(5), 337–358.

Sherman, Chris, & Price, Gary. (2001). *Invisible Web: Uncovering information sources search engines can't see* (1st ed.). Chicago: Independent Publishers Group.

CHAPTER 4

Visual Evaluation

The ARPAnet, the original Internet, was developed to connect universities working on government projects. Gradually, a series of networks developed in the United States, including Usenet and BITNET, to connect more colleges. Eventually, all these various networks became interconnected and the Internet was born. The not-very-exciting black-and-white text orientation and serious nature of the early Internet made it unattractive to commercial interests. However, once the World Wide Web added point-and-click visual interfaces and graphics with video and audio capability, the Internet began to resemble familiar mass media, such as television and newspapers. As a result, the context of the Internet began to change; visually distinguishing between serious, academic, and commercial online information became much more difficult.

Currently, there is no gatekeeping or editorial review of information on the Internet. Almost anyone can design websites to express a point of view, whether positive or negative, good or bad. For example, serious concern is being raised about the growing number of hate speech sites on the Internet. Hate speech spreads racial bigotry, Holocaust denial, gay bashing, and other offensive and, sadly, sometimes deadly points of view, such as those of the white supremacist groups Aryan Nations, the Ku Klux Klan, and Resistance

Records, a white-power record company. Some hate sites are professionally designed and contain strong visual logo elements that reflect the opinions expressed in the site. In addition to identifying websites with strongly biased content, savvy students also know how to recognize the visual manipulation techniques used by commercial web designers to capture your attention and distract you from a productive information search.

COMMERCIALIZATION ON THE WEB

Advertising is an integral part of mass media in the United States. It is through the revenues of advertising dollars that broadcast media survive to bring you popular programs such as *Survivor* or *Who Wants to Be a Millionaire?* Similarly, newspapers and magazines sell space to advertisers to help offset publishing costs. As the Web grew, it was made more attractive by graphical interfaces, and became present in more homes and businesses. The Web's graphic capabilities also attracted advertising and commercial sponsors. In the early days of radio and television, individual sponsors paid for the programming and in exchange they received air time to promote their products. Moreover, sponsoring a popular program helped create a positive image for the corporation. Today, companies such as Microsoft help sponsor educational sites on the Web. Sites with corporate sponsors generally feature a link to the sponsor's website.

One difference between traditional TV or radio commercials and web advertising is that in the past, the viewer or listener did not have to do anything to see or hear the ads. Web advertising is different because you have to type in the URL (or click on a pop-up ad) to visit a commercial website. Web companies have developed many (mostly annoying!) strategies, including **push technology,** for getting the unsuspecting web surfer to visit their sites. An input device, the Cue Cat, which reads URL "bar codes" with one swipe, has been given away by the millions to make it easier for you to visit commercial sites.

The commercialization of websites is becoming more sophisticated as pop-up advertisements are more commonly used. A software product called **Gator** has been challenged for its practice called "drive-by-downloads." This is a scheme in which a normal **banner ad** or pop-up ad will try to get a user to unknowingly install software on his or her computer. The primary purpose of this software is to load an advertising spyware module that displays pop-up advertisements when visiting some websites. The software is always running and it can spam users with special offers and display ads from competitors' sites.

Commercial activity on the Web can be placed into six categories: on-line storefront, Internet presence, content, mall, incentive site, and search engine. You may be surprised to see search engines listed as a commercial category in Chapter 1, but it is difficult not to notice the intrusive ads that are popping up on most web search engines, ads which are actually commercial sites that sell advertising space. For example, Yahoo! has an arrangement with Amazon.com to provide links to the Amazon site to purchase books.

Chapter 1 described a variety of different types of websites. Online storefronts enable people to purchase products directly through the Internet. In contrast, Internet presence sites provide a virtual presence for companies. Content sites are both free and fee based. Fee-based sites enable users to purchase information. For example, *The New York Times* (www.nytimes.com) provides free access to some content but charges users to download back-file articles for a fee. Other sponsored content sites, such as CNN (www.cnn.com), provide free online content to users. Malls are collections of online storefronts. Incentive sites pull users to the site by offering a contest, prize, or reason why people should access the site. These sites are created to help marketers generate traffic on their site. For example, Iwon.com is a search engine that gives away money as a way to increase its Internet traffic and Yahoo! and Google offer free email addresses. Search engines are often advertiser sponsored and popularity driven. See Chapter 2 for a list of the best ones to use.

JOURNALISM ON THE WEB

More and more, the Web is becoming a visual medium. There are a wide range of online journalism sites available on the Internet. Some are filled with pictures, video clips, and sound bites, while others are more text oriented. As stated in Chapter 1, text is frequently filled with misinformation. Spreading misinformation can be detrimental to a journalist's career. Recently there have been a number of news stories that have exposed the mis-reporting of information. Some reporters have even lost their jobs! Moreover, they have embarrassed their employers. Today, news sites need to be evaluated for their quality of information.

As more people turn to the Internet as a source of news information, the Internet is becoming a fourth news medium along with print, radio, and television. **Online journalism** can be viewed in two different ways. First, the Internet can be used as a reporting tool for stories distributed through traditional media. Second, the Internet can be used as a medium for news distribution. Deuze (2003) identifies four categories of online journalism: mainstream news sites, index and category sites, meta and comment sites, and share and discussion sites.

A widespread form of online news media is the mainstream news site, which is often associated with a traditional mass news medium. Examples of mainstream news sites are BBC, CNN, and MSNBC. These sites present editorial content with a minimal amount of filtered or moderated participatory communication created by web users. Index and category sites are associated with search engines (Yahoo!), agencies (Newsindex), and creative individuals (Drudge Report). These sites are characterized by having annotated editorials and links to other existing sites. Journalistic blogs can fall into this category.

Journalistic blogs were brought to the attention of students during the Second Gulf War. However, many students don't know that the Internet also played a role in the First Gulf War because one of the first books published from email messages was *Notes from a Sealed Room*, written by Robert Werman and edited by Gerald M. Phillips. Werman's email messages were written from inside a bomb shelter located in Israel and they told the story of waiting for explosions, Skud attacks, and air strikes. This book foreshadowed the role the Internet would play in the second war. During the Second Gulf War hundreds of journalists were embedded with the American military forces. On top of reporting for their news companies, some journalists started writing their own war blogs and distributing them on the Internet. In addition to traditional journalists, a number of web users began scanning war news, commentary, and information and they compiled this material into their own blogs. The appeal of the war blog was that it presented opinionated, but interesting, current event stories.

The third category of online journalism is meta- and comment sites. These sites comment on the news media and general news stories. Examples include mediachannel.org (see Figure 4.1) and Freedomforum. Alternative media sites, such as Guerilla News Network and Independent Media Centers, are also included in this category.

The final group of online journalism sites is share and discussion sites. These sites help meet the need for people to connect with one another (see Barnes, 2001). On share and discussion sites people exchange ideas, stories, and views on different topics. Sometimes these sites are called "group web logs." Online news sites fall into categories that range from mostly editorial content (mainstream news sites) to public connectivity-based sites (share and discussion sites). In addition to presenting news, online journalism sites balance content with connectivity.

FIGURE 4.1 Online journalism is on the rise. Mediachannel.org is an example of a site that comments about media.

Reprinted with permission from mediachannel.org.

Here are some actions that you should consider taking when evaluating a news website:

- Identify the type of news site; is it a traditional site or a personal blog?
- Look at the way terms are defined.
- Be aware of generalist language and underlying assumptions.
- Critique the types of supporting evidence being presented in the article.
- Identify facts versus opinions.
- Look for balanced reporting of both sides of an issue.

- Be aware of omissions in the article.
- Evaluate the writing style and logic of the article.

Using the Internet as an information tool has speeded up the reporting process. As a result, journalists sometimes report stories without fully checking their sources. So, this means that even news sites need to be carefully evaluated for possibilities of misinformation.

VISUAL PRESENTATION

Creating web-based presentations requires authors to think about how to present information in a way that is both visually engaging and interactive. **Graphical user interfaces** enable computer users to interact with both visual and text-based icons, and hypertext enables web authors to connect web pages interactively. Today, students can easily add pictures and graphics to their word-processed assignments. But few students have been taught the visual literacy skills used to create effective visual presentations. Consequently, students can become side-tracked by fancy graphics, animations, and the visual look of a website.

We live in a world full of visual media—television, newspapers, magazines, and billboards—filled with messages that fight for our attention. Designers use numerous visual techniques to capture our interest. These techniques include layout, color, movement, typography, and usability. Laying out art and copy on a page is a visual skill. The task is to place a variety of elements into an eye-catching and unified relationship. Some aesthetic principles from the fine arts, such as balance, contrast, and proportion, apply to web design.

To create balanced layouts, designers often place visual and verbal elements on a grid (see Figure 4.2). The grid provides a framework for a wide variety of different designs because placing images on several modular units and leaving other modules white creates contrast. In web design, a grid structure can be developed using table features. Visual and verbal information can be arranged in tables to create a balanced look for web pages (Figure 4.3). According to Dondis (1973), balance has important psychological and physical influences on human perception. To the receiver of visual information, the lack of balance and regularity is a disorienting factor. Therefore, information is better received when it is placed in a balanced layout.

FIGURE 4.2 Many designers use a basic grid system to organize elements on a page. Pictures, text, and graphics are placed in different areas of the grid to create a balanced layout.

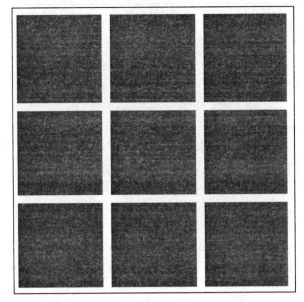

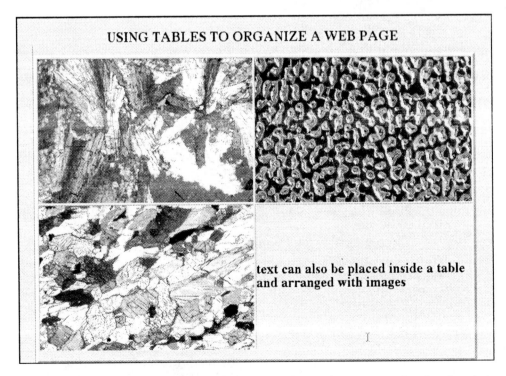

USING TABLES TO ORGANIZE A WEB PAGE

text can also be placed inside a table and arranged with images

FIGURE 4.3 When creating web pages, tables can be used to arrange visual and verbal elements into a gridlike layout. Marie L. Radford's personal home page also uses this technique.

Color

Colors also convey meanings that reinforce verbal messages. Warm colors—red, yellow, and orange—attract more attention than cool colors—blue, green, and purple. In addition to having different levels of attraction, colors also convey cultural meanings. Jan V. While (1990) describes an example in the following passage:

> Innumerable surveys have been made, and studying and understanding reaction to color is an important science, because purveyors of goods and services rely on these reactions to succeed in the marketplace. There are some useful pointers, for instance:
>
> Sugar is never packaged in green, because green carries connotations of sourness. It is packaged in blue, because blue is a color we associate with sweetness (p. 22).

The implied meaning associated with colors can also help communicate an idea. For example, in web design, black is the normal default color for text and blue text usually indicates a hypertext link. By clicking on the blue type, another page is accessed. After selecting a blue text link, the color of the text changes to purple to indicate that the link has already been chosen. Although this is a traditional color scheme, some web designers are experimenting with other color combinations to show a user that a link has been selected.

The colors a web designer uses can help to set a tone for the page. When viewing a website, check to see whether the colors support the verbal information being presented. For instance, does the site use basic default colors (blue and black text with a grey background) to present basic information? If the site features green, does it discuss nature, money, financial issues, or gardening tips? If the site uses a black background with reversed white type, is it presenting a serious topic or issue? If the colors and the message conflict, the site can seem less credible.

TIP
Remember the saying, "You can't judge a book by its cover"? The same holds true for websites. You can't always judge the quality of information on a site by its graphics alone.

DON'T JUDGE A WEBSITE BY ITS PRODUCTION VALUES

The Web is a visual medium and judging websites also requires you to be visually alert. Professional designers know how to direct your attention toward graphic elements and how to create the illusion of credibility. However, great-looking websites may not be the best source of information. In contrast to traditional mass media with professional writers and editors, just about anyone can create a website and make it available on the network. Many sites, such as virtual libraries, are not designed by professional graphic artists. Instead librarians create virtual library sites. Virtual library sites may have low visual appeal, but the information they contain is highly valuable.

Similarly, the use of online visual and verbal metaphors can be confusing. For example, both academic institutions and commercial companies use the virtual library metaphor. The metaphor of a library online obviously parallels visiting one and most of our physical libraries are nonprofit or educational establishments. However, unlike physical libraries, some virtual ones are being set up by corporations and commercial companies. Don't assume that all the information you access through a virtual library is legitimate. Some of these sites have been established with the purpose of distributing a specific type of information; all points of view may not be represented. Moreover, the information accessible on a commercial virtual library site could reflect a bias of the company that supports it.

Developing Visual Savvy

Being visually aware requires you to identify the **visual hierarchy** of a website, which is a group of visual (and verbal) elements arranged according to emphasis. Emphasis is achieved with contrast, stressing the relative importance, separation, or connection of graphic elements (see Figure 4.4). Visual hierarchies are created to enhance the overall purpose of the message being communicated. For example, to create a visual hierarchy on a business website, the designer must decide which component is the most important, is less important, and is the least important. The purpose of a visual hierarchy is to focus the eye on the most important component of the message being communicated.

As previously stated, colors can be used both to reinforce a verbal message and to divert our attention. Contrast between colors on a page both draws attention to page elements and enhances readability. According to web designer Roger Black, in order of importance, the first color is white, the second color is black, and the third color is red. White is the best background color because black holds the highest contrast to white. The contrast between black and white makes pages easier to read. For example, web designers who are concerned with legibility issues avoid problematic color choices, such as putting yellow type on orange backgrounds, because not enough contrast exists between the type and the background to read the text

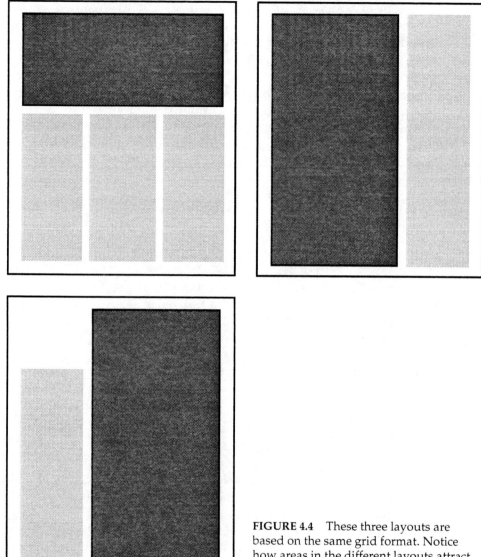

FIGURE 4.4 These three layouts are based on the same grid format. Notice how areas in the different layouts attract your attention to create visual hierarchies.

easily. After white and black, the next important color is red. Red is nature's danger color; it attracts our attention. Roger Black (1997) says, "Red is perfect. Red headlines sell magazines on newsstands twice as much as any other color" (p. 36).

In addition to visual hierarchies and color, animation also attracts our attention. When designers place moving images on a page, they automatically grab our attention. It comes as no surprise that web advertisers are aware of the impact of movement on a web page, and many advertising banners are deliberately designed to pull our attention away from the content of a site. Clicking on the banner takes you to another page of advertising that is specifically designed to persuade you to purchase a product or service. The impact of eye movement on web pages has been studied by Sheree Josephson (2004) with eye-tracking equipment. She found that location was the strongest variable in determining whether or not a user would look at a banner ad. Users were also visually attracted to banner ads with animations and moving graphics.

Graphics and Visual Interest

Text, images, and color can set a mood or tone for a website. For example, sites using the default colors of black type, blue links, and grey or white backgrounds imply a basic look or the idea of plain information. People who want to make information available on the Web and are not concerned about graphics might want to use this basic approach. Moreover, a fancy, colorful site that attracts your attention might be full of advertising and contain very little useful information.

Given the option of going to a website that is predominantly text based or one that is filled with graphics and video, most students choose the latter. However, sites with movie clips and sound clips are generally promotional sites that do not provide any serious information because they are designed to sell a media product. Moving graphics are generally not used by reference and digital library sites. Three reasons explain why. First, digital video takes a long time to download to a computer screen. Second, video images take up a tremendous amount of space or bandwidth, which makes them slow memory hogs. Finally, animations can detract students away from the important textual information located on the site.

Sites that contain scholarly information are often text oriented; their designers use graphics cautiously. An exception to this rule is educational medical and scientific sites that include visual simulations to explain complex concepts. Some of these sites use graphics effectively both to capture attention and to communicate ideas.

GRAPHIC EVALUATION OF WEBSITES

Today the Internet is filled with graphics and advertising that can distract the student from his or her research. Although many of us tune out commercials on television, the same is not always true about commercialism on the Web. The following are some graphic questions that you should consider when evaluating the presentation of websites:

1. Is the graphic designed to capture your attention?
2. Is the image being used as a form of visual persuasion to make you think or feel a certain way?
3. What type of emotional message does it convey?
4. Does the image complement and support the text?
5. Does the site use a visual metaphor and does it support the content?

Commercial Manipulation Strategies

The visual manipulation strategies used in commercial advertising are now being applied to websites. Some sites visually resemble older media and their advertising techniques are obvious. In contrast, other sites are incorporating new types of programming and animation tricks to grab attention and manipulate how people browse the Web. On many sites, you have to click through pages of advertising to find any information. In the worst cases, advertising pops up in a window that covers the page. You have to close this window before you can access information on the site.

Good web design takes you to relevant information within three mouse clicks; in contrast, manipulative designs trap you in the site. In web marketing, *client pull* is the technique of taking over a viewer's browser to take him or her to a website the designer wants the viewer to see. For example, when designers use the HTML programming code called META, the code tells the browser to go to the next page in the site, or to go back and forth among the pages within that site. This simple programming trick can trap you in a website, dragging you deeper and deeper into the site with no apparent escape.

A number of websites are **portal sites,** which are designed to attract mass audiences. These sites include the search engine Yahoo! The home page of a portal site is designed to get people deeper and deeper into the site. Instead of browsing the many different sites on the Internet, these sites want people to stay or "stick" with their site. Therefore, they are designed to keep you locked in the site and they discourage you from leaving. For example, when using Yahoo! as a search engine, you may have to click several times through different screens before you reach a list of links to other sites. While you are clicking, the advertising banner at the top of the page changes to an advertisement that relates to the topic you are searching.

Although Yahoo! is a popular search engine, it is also a commercial site that is carefully designed to make you notice its advertising so it can continue to attract sponsors. Understanding how web images and icons are used to manipulate and persuade will make you a more effective web researcher and less likely to be distracted by pushy ploys.

A fun Internet prank is to create a parody of an existing website. Just as *Saturday Night Live* pokes fun at politicians and celebrities, creators of these parody sites poke fun at other websites. For example, there are two parody sites for the official White House website (www.whitehouse.gov). You can reach these sites by typing in www.whitehouse.net or www.whitehouse.org. Another site that is often made fun of is the Drudge Report (www.drudgereport.com). Try typing in www.drudge.com and see if you'll find the "Drudge Retort." Another way to test your parody detection skills is to evaluate www.dhmo.org and www.malepregnancy.com. Is either one of these sites a parody site? What do you think?

Have you ever missed class because a couple of minutes of web surfing turned into a couple of hours? When doing web research, don't get sidetracked by pushy advertisements and manipulative graphics.

INFORMATION NAVIGATION

A central characteristic of the Web is **hypertext,** which links together information and pages. **Internal links** connect pages within a website. **External links** connect pages from different websites. Links are indicated by text and graphics, including underlined words, phrases, visual icons, and audio-clips. As you navigate the Web, the arrow icon changes to a pointing finger when it passes over a link. Selecting different links to navigate information space is a key method for accessing web information.

Navigation and Nontext Features

Graphical browsers add many nontext features to help students navigate the Internet. These include icons, logos, maps, photographs, sounds, and video files. Arrows, buttons, and scrolling bars are visual features used by web designers. These icons enable users to navigate a website and access information.

Navigational aids help students find information on the Web. For instance, an arrow pointing to the right moves one page forward; an arrow pointing to the left moves one page backward (see Figure 4.4). Other navigation features include the title tag, links, navigation icons, and a site map. Every web page has a short and descriptive name. Depending on the browser, this title either appears in the title bar of the window or on the top of the screen. In addition to describing the page, the title is used in indexes and bookmarks. Search engines pick up the title of the site as its default description.

As previously discussed, hypertext links are underlined text, iconic buttons, or link **anchors** that connect related pieces of information. For instance, links often connect to information that defines a term or provides more information about a particular topic. Similarly, anchors also are used for text navigation because they take readers to sections of a text located on the web page. Links can connect to information located within a single site or they can connect a site to other web pages located anywhere on the global network.

Site maps and indexes can also help users navigate web information. Site maps present a visual representation of the location of information on the site. These maps are often linked to the sections of the site that are represented on the map. An index is an alphabetical listing of the major components of a website. An index or site map provides a quick overview of the site and enables students to locate information more easily.

Evaluation of Navigation Design

Websites should be designed for easy access to relevant information. Sites designed with the intention of making information easily accessible make the amount of content located on the site clearly known. Additionally, the type of information available should be organized into logical units or document groups to help you find the materials that are located on the site. Moreover, the purpose and goals of the site should be clearly articulated. The following are critical content questions to ask when evaluating a site:

1. Is the volume of information contained on the site clearly indicated?
2. Is information on the site grouped into logical units?
3. Does the site have an obvious visual hierarchy? What is the relationship between elements?
4. Does the site indicate which reference materials are located on the site and which ones are on other sites?
5. Are goals articulated for the various areas of the site?
6. Are full texts or only abstracts available?

7. Does the site contain large graphics or visual elements that take time to download?

8. Is the site a digital library collection or a commercial information site?

Many web designers consider oversized graphics the number one sign of poor web design. Graphics should be kept small in size to accommodate a variety of different modem speeds. But there are some exceptions to this rule. Libraries and art collections are now making their collections available online, and large-image collections can take time to download. Digital library collections include the Vatican Library (lcweb.loc.gov/exhibits/vatican/toc.html), the IBM/Andrew Wyeth Project (www.almaden.ibm.com/u/gladney/antiquit.htm), the rare book site at Yale University Beinecke (www.library.yale.edu/beinecke), and the Library of Congress website (www.loc.gov). To protect the copyright of these images, digital library collections frequently place a watermark or embossed logo on the image. Watermarked images indicate that the material on the site is owned by the sponsoring organization. The images are available for viewing, but they cannot be downloaded or printed. Watermarks tend to indicate that the site is presenting original images with a high level of authenticity.

INTERACTIVE FUNCTIONALITY EVALUATION AND USABILITY

The ability to find information easily with several mouse clicks is an indication that a site is designed for interactive functionality. Moreover, well-designed sites have escape links to take you back to the home page of the site. When doing a search, you can end up in the middle of a site. Look for a visual or verbal link to the site's home page to find out more information about who is sponsoring the site and why. If you can't find a link or more information, the information should be checked against another source. The following are critical questions based on design functionality:

1. Does the site follow web conventions? For example, is the text black with blue links?

2. Can you find information quickly with three mouse clicks?

3. Does the site provide its own internal search engine to help you locate information?

4. Can you navigate the site easily?

5. Do the visual images help you better navigate the site?

6. Does the site provide an index or site map?

7. Does every page have a link back to the home page of the site? Can you exit the site?

8. Does each page have an identifying name (or logo), date, and contact email address?

Creating a website that balances interactive functionality and visual design can be difficult. For example, librarians who create sites often have to choose between overloading a page with information or organizing it into units that require additional mouse clicks to access relevant information. Consequently, some highly legitimate sites that contain valuable information are not visually appealing. For example, the Refdesk (www .refdesk.com) is crowded and unattractive, but the links are carefully chosen and of high quality. On the surface some valuable sites may not attract your attention. You have to read the text carefully or scroll down the screen to use the site functionally.

Usability

Bringing all of the elements together—graphics, text, navigation, and functionality—into a web design that is easy for you to navigate is the goal of usability design. For instance, **universal usability** is defined as the ability of "more than 90 percent of all households being successful users of information and communication technologies at least once a week" (Shneiderman, 2002, p. 36). Usability tends to focus on the engineering side of software design, rather than the artistic side. In contrast to graphic artists who look at the aesthetics of a web page, usability designers study users and how they work with web pages (see Nielsen, 2000). A key principle of usability is simplicity in web design. The following is a list of reasons why websites often fail the usability test:

- Treating the Web like a brochure rather than a new medium
- Structuring a site to mirror a company rather than the way a user would access information
- Creating a gorgeous looking web page for company approval instead of creating an optimal user experience
- Writing in a linear style for the printed page rather than a style that is geared for the hypermediated Web

- Considering your site to be a standalone site without linking to other relevant sites

The preceding list could be turned around into questions to evaluate the usability of a site. But, common sense will tell you whether or not a website passes the usability test. The basic question is as follows: Can you easily perform the tasks you want to achieve when visiting a site?

SUMMARY

In this chapter you read about

- Commercialization on the Web
- Journalism on the Web
- Some basic tips for visual presentation, including
    How color captures attention and conveys meaning
    Using grid formats as a design framework
    The importance of balance in layout
- Points for developing visual savvy, including
    Becoming visually alert
    Identifying a site's visual hierarchy to note emphasis
    Becoming aware of the use of color, animation, and graphics to grab attention
    Becoming aware of manipulation strategies, such as trapping users in a website, that commercial sites use to promote a product or service
- Tips for evaluating information design, including
    Nonverbal navigation elements
    Ascertaining whether the content design of a site is fluff or substantive
    Determining whether the interactive functionality of a site makes it easy to navigate or to find what you are looking for
- Usability

WEB DESIGN SITES

General
12 Web Page Design Decisions for Business and Organizations
www.wilsonweb.com/articles/12design.htm

Style Guide for Online Hypertext
www.w3.org/Provider/Style/Overview.html

Web Page Design for Designers
www.wpdfd.com/wpdhome.htm

What Makes a Good Home Page
www.werbach.com/web/page_design.html

Universal Design (Handicap Issues)
Trace: Designing a More Usable Word for All
www.trace.wisc.edu/world

Examples of Bad Web Design and Design Mistakes
Top 10 Mistakes in Web Design
www.useit.com/alertbox/9605.html

Online Journalism

www.cnn.com
news.bbc.co.uk
www.nsnbc.com
www.yahoo.com
www.drudgereport.com

www.mediachannel.org
www.freedomforum.org
www.gnn.tv
www.indymedia.org

Usability Websites

www.useit.com
www.useit.com/alertbox
semanticstudios.com
www.usableweb.com

www.w3.org
www.w3.org/WAI/gettingstarted
builder.com

BIBLIOGRAPHY FOR FURTHER READING

Alexander, Janet E., & Tate, Marsha Ann. (1999). *Web wisdom: How to evaluate and create information quality on the Web.* Mahwah, NJ: Lawrence Erlbaum.

Allen, N. (2002). *Working with words and images.* Westport, CT: Ablex Publishing.

Barry, Ann Marie Seward. (1997). *Visual intelligence: Perception, image, and manipulation in visual communication.* Albany: State University of New York Press.

Berger, Arthur Asa. (1998). *Seeing is believing.* (2nd ed.). Mountain View, CA: Mayfield Press.

Cali, D. D. (2000). The logic of the link: The associative paradigm in communication criticism. *Critical Studies in Media Communication, 17*(4), 397–408.

Cannon, C. M. (2001, April). The real computer virus. *American Journalism Review, 23*(3), 28–35.

Deuze, M. (2003). The web and its journalisms: Considering the consequences of different types of newsmedia online. *New Media & Society, 5*(2), 203–230.

Diaper, D., & Waelend, P. (2000). World Wide Web working whilst ignoring graphics: Good news for web page designers. *Interacting with Computers, 13,* 163–181.

Dondis, Donis A. (1973). *A primer for visual literacy.* Cambridge: The MIT Press.

Fox, E. A., & Marchionini, G. (Eds.). (2001, May). Digital libraries. *Association for Computing Machinery, 44*(5), 30–33.

Fraim, J. (2002). Electronic symbols: Internet words and culture. *First Monday, Vol. 7, No. 6.* Retrieved November, 23, 2004, from firstmonday.org/issues/issue7_6/fraim/index.html

Harrison, T. M., & Stephen, T. (1996). *Computer networking and scholarly communication in the twenty-first-century university.* Albany: State University of New York Press.

Jackson, B., & Jamieson, K. H. (2004). Finding fact in political debates. *American Behavioral Scientist, 48*(2), 229–237.

Johnson-Eilola, J. (2002). *Designing effective web sites.* New York: Houghton Mifflin Company.

Josephson, S. (2004). Eye tracking methodology and the Internet. In K. Smith, S. Moriarty, G. Barbatsis, & K. Kenney, eds., *Handbook of visual communication* (pp. 63–80). Mahwah, NJ: Lawrence Earlbaum Associates.

McKinley, T. (1997). *From paper to web: How to make information instantly accessible.* San Jose, CA: Adobe Press.

Meggs, Philip B. (1989). *Type and image: The language of graphic design.* New York: Van Nostrand Reinhold.

Nielson, J. (2000). *Designing web usability.* Indianapolis, IN: New Riders Publishing.

Papson, S., Goldman, R., & Kersey, N. (2004). Web site design. *American Behavioral Scientist, 47*(12), 1617–1643.

Pavlik, J. (2001). *Journalism and new media.* New York: Columbia University Press.

Peek, R. P., & Newby, G. B. (1996). *Scholarly publishing: The electronic frontier.* Cambridge: The MIT Press.

Shneiderman, B. (2002). *Leonardo's laptop: Human needs and the new computing technologies.* Cambridge, MA: MIT Press.

Waters, C. (1996). *Web concept and design: A comprehensive guide for creating effective web sites.* Indianapolis, IN: New Riders Publishing.

Weinman, L. (1996). *Designing web graphics. 2: How to prepare images and media for the web.* Indianapolis, IN: New Riders Publishing.

Werman, R. (1993). *Notes from a sealed room.* Carbondale, IL: Southern Illinois University Press.

White, Jan V. (1990). *Color for the electronic age.* New York: Watson-Guptill Publishers.

CHAPTER 5

Copyright Issues and the Web

Suppose you worked really hard on a creative project, perhaps wrote a song, made a music video, wrote a short story, or devised a great new computer game. Then, suppose someone came along and took your story, song, video, or game and made it available to anyone and everyone in the world, free of charge, with *no* credit or profit for you. This scenario, of course, would be a good example of what is commonly known as being ripped off! Well, this is what is happening anytime someone downloads or copies information from the Web without giving the author proper credit or citing their source.

"Music sampling is fun, but when writing a paper, cutting and pasting from Internet pages is not cool! More profs. are using cheater detection software to catch students who copy from the Web."

In the United States, people have the right to be compensated for their creative work. As a result, **copyright** laws have been established to protect every author's intellectual property, including written work, photographs, illustrations, music, and videos. Copyright owners have the exclusive right to copy, distribute, display, and transmit their intellectual property. Permission can be granted to others to use the work, and, in some cases, works are "licensed." Licensing gives others the right to copy and distribute the work within stipulated guidelines. The highly publicized lawsuit against Napster, the popular music-swapping website, argues that the site has been distributing copyrighted material without permission from the copyright owners. As a result, a number of copyright owners have sued Napster. The moral of the story is, if you want to use the creative work of other people, you need to get their permission first. However, the rules of "fair use" constitute an exception to the copyright law.

STAY OUT OF TROUBLE WITH FAIR-USE GUIDELINES

A fair-use exemption creates a limited set of conditions that allow people to use a copyrighted work without first obtaining permission from the copyright owner. Think about the previous scenario, in which someone took your creative work and distributed it without your permission and without compensation. Wouldn't you be happy to have your work distributed as long as you said it was okay? And, even better, wouldn't it be great to get paid every time someone else used or copied your work? Well, central to the idea of fair use is the notion that your particular use of the work does not divert income from the creator nor influence their potential future income.

Although creative work can be copyright protected, ideas cannot. Therefore, you can write about something someone has already discussed or published. However, using direct quotes or portions of a published work requires giving the author credit. Exemptions under the fair-use interpretation of copyright law are allowed when

- Only a small amount of the copyrighted work is being used
- The small amount used is only an unimportant portion of the entire work and does not define its essence
- The copyright work is being used for educational purposes
- The use of the copyrighted work does not affect the copyright holder's ability to receive income from the work

As you can see, the interpretation of fair use could be tricky. What constitutes educational purposes, for example? How can you tell whether the part of the work you are using is not its essence? Copyright laws are often misunderstood. Many copyright violations take place by those who mistakenly (and often with good intentions) believe that they have the right to make copies.

For example, you paid for an expensive word processing program and installed it on your computer. Your girlfriend or boyfriend asks you to install the program on her/his computer too, *for educational purposes* (i.e., to do homework assignments). Do you think this is a violation of copyright? You might rationalize installing it in this way: "I paid for the program. I want to be able to use it at my significant other's room or apartment. Why shouldn't I install it there, too?" However, you would be in violation of copyright because your installation of that program results in a lack of sale of that program to your main squeeze and a loss of income to the author/software producer.

Many battles, over many years, fought in U.S. courts, have resulted in some clarification of the gray areas in copyright laws (see the U.S. Copyright Office website at www.copyright.gov). However, the introduction of digital property, and now the Web, has introduced even grayer areas, and copyright laws have not kept pace with electronic developments. Although most of the information presented through the Web is copyright protected, there is a common belief that messages posted to a public group can be freely copied and distributed. Graphics, sound bites, and text that are copied from websites can be violations of the copyright law. Students creating web pages mistakenly believe that copyright-protected images (such as the Simpsons cartoon characters, or registered company logos) can be cut and pasted into their sites without the creator's permission. These students are wrong!

DON'T ABUSE FAIR USE

Fair use is for educational contexts. Student home pages do not necessarily fall into this category. Students who do not understand how the copyright law works often violate the law without realizing it. For instance, Dale A. Herbeck and Christopher D. Hunter (2001) examined 400 student-authored web pages and discovered that 43 percent of the images used on student pages belonged to someone else. They identified three different ways in which students tend to infringe on other people's copyright:

1. The blatant use of materials that include a visible mark of protection, such as copyright ©, reserved ®, or trademarked TM seals. Examples of this category include cartoon characters and sports logos.

2. The use of materials that are probably protected but do not use a copyright mark. Examples include sports photographs, album and compact disk covers, television characters, and company logos.

3. The use of school or university photographs, seals, logos, shields, and mascots. Although some universities may encourage students to use these images, they do belong to the university, and students should use these materials with caution.

Several steps can be taken to make sure you are using images properly. The best way to protect oneself is to ask for permission to use the material. Requests can be snail mailed or emailed to the copyright owners. The following sample is a letter of request:

Date

Address [If mailed]

Dear _____:

May I have permission to include your [photograph, illustration, article] in my [project, book, website]? Use of your materials will in no way restrict republication of your material in any other form by you or others authorized by you. A release form is provided below.

I (we) grant the permission requested. The undersigned has the right to grant the permission requested herein and the material does not infringe upon the copyright of other rights of third parties. The undersigned is the owner/author of such materials.

Credit Line to be given: _____

_____

_____

Name _____ Date _____

GUIDELINES FOR OBTAINING PERMISSION

In general, if you want to use someone else's work, you need to get their permission. You should ask for permission in the following cases:

- When using more than 500 words from any single printed source, including all quotations
- When quoting more than 8 percent of a work

- When using any recent artwork or photograph from another source, unless it is a copyright-free image (discussed next)
- When quoting lines from a song or poem

However, some people want their work on the Internet to be shared, and they include permission statements at the end of their work. An example follows:

© 2000, Pat Doe. Permission is granted to freely copy and distribute in electronic or printed form for nonprofit and educational purposes only. The author retains all other rights. If you have any questions, please contact the creator, at patdoe@coldmail.com.

When you see this statement, the materials can be copied and distributed for educational use without directly contacting the owner of the copyright.

CREATIVE COMMONS

An alternative to fair-use and copyright law is now being explored by the Creative Commons nonprofit corporation. The corporations aim to develop a new type of reasonable copyright that will enable content creators to express themselves and build upon others' work. Creative Commons is developing a series of licensing options that are beyond the freedoms of fair use and more flexible than the extremes to "All" or "No" copyright protection. Under this new type of licensing, content is marked with the CC mark and the content creator chooses a license from a variety of choices. For more information on using **Creative Commons licensing** go to www.creativecommons.org to view the copyright licensing options.

COPYRIGHT FOR THE WEB
AND A DIGITAL MILLENNIUM

The Web is a global medium. Different countries have different copyright laws. The Digital Millennium Copyright Act of 1998 makes the United States copyright laws conform to two treaties adopted by the World Intellectual Property Organization

(WIPO). Basically, all countries have to offer copyright protection to foreign works of **intellectual property** and the protection must be at least as strong as the protection for works in the native country. Moreover, all countries must attempt to prevent using technology to circumvent copyright laws.

What does this mean to you? Information service providers, such as America Online (AOL) and the Microsoft Network, must reject customers that they know engage in copyright infringement. As soon as an Internet service provider receives a complaint of infringement, it must take steps to remove the material from the online service. Under this law, copyright owners also have the right to demand information about the individual who violated copyright.

Copyright Exceptions!

Exceptions to copyright law include works in the public domain and copyright-free clip art. Copyright does not last forever; all works eventually return to the public domain. This means that the images are free for anyone to use. For example, the image of the Mona Lisa falls into this category, and people have used her image in a variety of ways, including adding a mustache! All this is perfectly legal because Mona's image is in the public domain. Works copyrighted before 1978 entered the public domain 75 years after their publication. Between 1978 and 1998, copyright was the life of the author plus 50 years. In 1998, the Sonny Bono Copyright Term Extension Act extended earlier copyright terms by 20 years. As a result of this Act, a large quantity of Disney material that would have gone into the public domain now still belongs to the Disney Company.

Materials for which copyright has expired are considered public domain. Caution! These materials are not current editions, but from much older editions. Examples of public domain materials can be found on the Web:

- *Bartlett's Familiar Quotations* (10th edition) at the Bartleby site, which features public domain works (www.bartleby.com/100)
- *Roget's Thesaurus* (www.thesaurus.com)

Copyright-free clip art and graphics also constitute exceptions to copyright law because the creators of the work intend for it to be shared. A number of free clip-art services are available on the Web. The good news is that these sites have been linked together into a graphics **web ring** to enable you to click back and forth easily between sites. The bad news is that these sites are filled with annoying advertising banners, windows, and graphics. But after breaking through the clutter, you can find images that do not violate anyone's copyright. Copyright-free art sites include

www.barrysclipart.com
www.free-clip-art.net
www.clipart-graphics.net
www.allclipartsite.com

Materials that were never copyrighted constitute yet another exception to copyright law. These materials include all publications of the U.S. Government Printing Office, which cannot by law be copyrighted. This explains the many versions in print of the Starr Report on former President Clinton and the various versions of the U.S. census.

Freedom of Information

As information is increasingly placed on the Web, the issue of access to information becomes more important. For example, a government can now provide public information in a digital format. Income tax forms and copies of other legal documents are now publically available online. Additionally, cities, towns, and states have all opened electronic dialogs with their citizens.

But, freedom of information plays an even larger role in American culture. Jessica Litman (2001) says, "Part of the information ethos in the United States is that facts and ideas cannot be owned, suppressed, censored, or regulated; they are meant to be found, studied, passed along, and freely traded in the 'marketplace of ideas'" (p. 11). A complex collection of information laws prescribe the conditions and terms in which content providers can distribute their work, including broadcasters, print-based publishers, advertisers, journalists, and web creators.

You need to understand the rules and regulations that apply to specific industries and professions. For example, through the **Freedom of Information Act** (FOIA), journalists and the public at large can get access to government documents. In 1966, Congress passed this act to give the public the right to discover information about federal agencies. Then in 1996, the Electronic Freedom of Information Act (EFOIA) was passed, making information available on the Internet. Today, many government agencies publish information, ranging from press releases to statistics on the Internet, in an electronic form.

Although the First Amendment protects freedom of speech on the Internet and in the press, broadcasters have language restrictions. Similarly, commercial free speech used by advertisers has more limitations than an individual's free speech rights. Even though freedom of speech exists on the Internet, students still need to be aware that much of the information on the Web is copyright protected and is not "free" for the taking. Improper use of on- and off-line copyright material can lead to plagiarism problems.

WEB CHEATING

Every college and university has rules against plagiarism. **Plagiarism** is using someone else's ideas and words without providing the proper citations or references. When students are caught cheating, consequences may include failing the assignment, failing the course, suspension, and sometimes expulsion. Examples of plagiarism follow:

- Recycling the papers of other students
- Purchasing a paper from a ghost writer
- Copying materials word for word from a book or journal article without citing the source
- Using ideas and passages of texts without acknowledging the author, without using quotation marks, or without including references

There are a variety of ways that students can engage in web cheating. For instance, Lisa Renard (1999/2000) identifies two types of Internet cheaters—sneaky and lazy. Sneaky cheaters are those who engage in cut-and-paste plagiarism, which is taking phrases, sentences, and paragraphs from a number of different websites and weaving them together into a paper. This style of cheating is also called patchwriting because it involves taking material from a source text and modifying it without citing the original reference. In contrast, lazy cheaters will order a paper from a paper mill or just download an entire piece from the Internet and say it is their own.

Re-mixing or sampling may work in music, but it doesn't apply to writing. Forgetting to place quotation marks and proper citations in your paper is technically a form of plagiarism. For instance, you can't legally just copy and paste sentences from different electronic sources to create a paper of your own.

Computer technology makes it easy to copy information and paste it into another document. It is an easy way for cheaters to plagiarize. However, sometimes even the most honest students working against a deadline can be careless about marking text after a cut and paste. Then they can lose track of where the quotation began and ended. Following are some tips to help you understand when you can and cannot use material copied from the Web for class projects.

DON'TS

- Don't buy papers from an online term-paper mill.
- Don't use a paper from a free term-paper site, such as School Sucks, Other People's Papers, or Evil House of Cheat (see the Tip below).
- Don't cut and paste without marking the text (use **bold** or *italics* to help keep track, or make a print-out of the web page for future reference).

DO'S

- Supply the proper citations and acknowledgments for web sources (see Chapter 6).
- Make sure quotation marks are placed around copied materials.
- Always make note of the web URL for your reference list and in case you need to return to verify material on the original web page.
- Make sure paraphrased materials also are properly acknowledged.

As easy as it is for students to copy papers off the Web, it is easier for professors to find them. In the past, detecting plagiarism required ingenuity, skill, and an amazing memory for text. Today, simply placing a few phrases in a good search engine can identify web cheating.

 ....

Let the Cheater BEWARE!

Term-paper websites promise to lighten your course load, and some even guarantee that they cannot be detected, all for a mere $7.95 per page. But is it really worth the price? Actually, this is false advertising. New software programs enable professors to catch cheaters, and those choosing to buy online papers may find themselves in deep trouble. For example, Glatt Plagiarism Services (www.plagiarism.com) is a program designed to spot recycled text.

Is Web Cheating Worth It?

As another semester was getting ready to start, Suzy Hansen, a *New York Times* reporter, decided to check out companies that sold term papers on the Web. After researching a dozen sites, she found many places to enable cheating on the Internet and decided to try two different types of sites. First, term papers can be purchased for anywhere between $20 and $45. Second, students can purchase a custom written paper for about $45 per page. So, she bought one of each and compared them. The prewritten paper was delivered almost immediately and it was terrible. It had run on sentences and a sloppy writing style that mimicked the writing patterns of a confused freshman. In contrast, the custom paper, which cost $180 and was delivered in three days, was much better. But, was it worth the money?

Wait, there's a dilemma. If you're a cheap cheat, the paper will be shoddy and teachers would believe you wrote it. If you're willing to cough-up the cash (or credit card) for a custom paper, the quality might raise a teacher's eyebrow. What a bind! Considering that it only takes a few hours to read a book and then a few more to write the paper, its amazing that students will risk their integrity, their education, and futures for these few hours of college time.

TIP

Before buying a paper from a cheat site, check the academic integrity guidelines of your university. Are the penalties worth the cheating risk? Maybe you should talk to your professor about a time extension before you risk your future.

Academic Integrity

The values of academic integrity are essential for successful college and working careers. The Center for Academic Integrity, a consortium of 200 universities, colleges, and educational organizations, has identified five fundamental values associated with academic integrity—honesty, trust, fairness, respect, and responsibility.

Honesty is at the center of academic integrity and colleges condemn cheating, lying, and fraud, along with dishonest behavior. Honesty is at the foundation of teaching, learning, and research. Students and teachers respond to honesty with trust. Teachers expect students to honestly write homework assignments and exams. In return, students require that teachers grade their work in a fair and honest way. This mutual trust creates an environment of fair and accurate evaluation, which is vital for all

levels of academic work, including scholarly books, articles, research and writing.

In addition to creating a learning environment built on mutual trust, teachers and students need to respect each other's work. Teachers show respect by honestly and fairly grading a student and by taking a student's ideas seriously. Students demonstrate respect by coming to class on time, paying attention, listening to the opinions of others, and by turning in honestly written papers and homework assignments. Building respect requires students and teachers to take shared responsibility. Every educational institution has procedures for students to take, if they honestly believe that a teacher has not treated them fairly. However, being a responsible student is not always easy. It can mean taking action against wrongdoing in the classroom, for example some college honor codes require that students report cheating during tests. Unlike teachers, students have greater peer pressure, fear, and loyalty issues to handle. (See the Center for Academic Integrity website [www.academicintegrity.org] for more information and a more detailed description of academic integrity.)

Education is based on honesty, trust, fairness, respect, and responsibility. For you to write papers honestly and respect the scholarly work and ideas of others, you need to learn how to follow copyright and fair use guidelines. But most important, you need to learn how to properly cite the work of others from both print-based and electronic formats, the subject of the next chapter.

Perceptions about Web Cheating

As times and technologies change, educators have become increasingly concerned about the impact of cyber-plagiarism. Some say that Internet plagiarism rose to 40 percent in 2003 (see Hansen, 2004), others argue that academic misconduct has risen to 90 percent (see Ercegovac & Richardson, 2004). Patrick Scanlon (2002) studied student online plagiarism and described some of the issues associated with using the Internet as a research tool. First, a new generation of students may be attempting to redefine the conception of "fair use." Students sometimes mistakenly think that freely shared information found on the Internet is public knowledge for use in any context. Stated another way, students growing up on the Internet tend to see text in cyberspace as free and theirs for the taking. Second, "students may be under the impression lifting information from the Internet, even verbatim, is good research practice rather than cheating" (Scanlon, 2002, p. 162). The misperception about cyber-text is that borrowing thoughts from a variety of Internet sources and assembling them into a final product is an acceptable way to write a college paper, but most professors do not agree because they consider this to be cut-and-paste plagiarism. Finally, Napster, Mozilla, and similar software programs that make it easy to copy and download music and films alter perceptions about copyright and ownership of electronic content. Just because something is available on the Internet does not mean that it is free for the taking. Misperceptions like these contribute to the act of cyber-plagiarism.

According to Scanlon and Neumann (2002) seven acts of plagiarism include the following:

- Copying text (without citation) and using it in a paper
- Copying (without citation) an entire paper
- Asking another person to give you an entire paper

- Using the Internet to cut and copy text (without citation) into a paper
- Using the Internet to copy a paper (without citation) and putting your name on it
- Purchasing a paper from an on- or off-line paper mill
- Going online to ask someone to give you a paper

So, why do students consider web cheating to be acceptable? One reason is that students don't clearly understand the idea of plagiarism. Therefore, it is suggested that teachers discuss the idea with their students. Moreover, studies (Scanlon & Neumann, 2002) have shown that peer pressure may be a key reason why students think that cheating is acceptable. Students tend to overestimate the amount of cheating their peers are doing. For example, 8 percent of the surveyed students self-reported that they had cut and pasted text from the Internet (without citations). But, 50.4 percent of the same students estimated that their peers cut and paste information. "In other words, if students perceive that a majority of their peers are going online to plagiarize, they may be more apt to plagiarize themselves" (Scanlon & Neumann, 2002).

Additionally, the academic community contributes to plagiarism by failing to communicate the value of independent scholarship and thoughtful thinking. Independent and creative thinking is a skill valued in academia and also in commercial industries. For instance, in addition to good verbal and writing skills, some companies are looking for creative problem-solvers to work in team-oriented workplaces.

When you copy and paste, remember to quote and cite. It is acceptable to use quotes from credible websites, you just have to remember to put the copied material inside quote marks and cite the website (see the next chapter for citation guidelines). A simple trick is to copy and paste the website address along with the quoted material.

SUMMARY

In this chapter you read about

- Copyright issues and the Web
- Creative commons Freedom of Information

- Fair-use guidelines and exemptions to copyright, including

  Using a small amount of the copyrighted work

  Using a nonessential portion of the copyrighted work

  Using copyrighted work for educational purposes

  Not affecting the copyright holder's potential income when using the copyrighted material

- Abuses of fair use, including

  Blatantly using materials (such as cartoons) that display a visible copyright or trademark seal

  Using materials that are probably protected (like logos) but do not have a copyright mark

  Using university or college seals or logos without checking to make sure it is permitted

- Guidelines for obtaining permission

  Using more than 500 words from a single source

  Quoting more than 8 percent of a work

  Using artwork or photographs that are not copyright-free clip art

  Quoting lines from a song or poem

- Copyright exceptions for works in the public domain and copyright-free clip art

- Do's and don'ts to avoid web cheating

- Academic integrity

- Perceptions about web cheating

COPYRIGHT WEBSITES
••••••••••••••••••••••••••••••••

Copyright Clearance Center
www.copyright.com

Copyright Resources on the Internet
groton.k12.ct.us/mts/pt2a.htm

**Regents Guide to Understanding
    Copyright and Educational Fair Use**
www.usg.edu/legal/copyright

U.S. Copyright Office
www.copyright.gov

U.S. Patents and Trademarks Office
www.uspto.gov

**World Intellectual Property
    Organization Treaties**
www.wipo.int

Plagiarism Software Programs

EVE2
www.canexus.com/eve

Glatt Plagiarism Program
www.plagiarism.com

Turnitin.com
www.turnitin.com

Academic Integrity

Avoiding Plagiarism
sja.ucdavis.edu/avoid.htm

The Center for Academic Integrity
www.academicintegrity.org/cai_research.asp

The Fundamental Values of Academic Integrity
www.academicintegrity.org/pdf/FVProject.pdf

Plagiarism: What It Is and How to Avoid It
www.indiana.edu/~wts/pamphlets/plagiarism.shtml

Plagiarism, Copyright, and Fair Use Tutorials and Testing

Avoiding Plagiarism
www.maricopa.edu/distance_learning/tutorials/study/plagiarism.shtml

Copyright Tutorial
www.lib.utsystem.edu/copyright

Creative Commons
www.creativecommons.org

Fair Use Harbor
www.stfrancis.edu/cid/copyrightbay/fairuse.htm

Paraphrase: Write It in Your Own Words
owl.english.purdue.edu/handouts/research/r_paraphr.html

Quoting, Paraphrasing, and Summarizing
owl.english.purdue.edu/handouts/research/r_quotprsum.html

A Visit to Copyright Bay
www.stfrancis.edu/cid/copyrightbay

BIBLIOGRAPHY FOR FURTHER READING

Callahan, D. (2004), *The cheating culture: Why more Americans are doing wrong to get ahead.* New York: Harcourt.

Casey, Timothy D. (2000). *ISP liability survival guide: Strategies for managing copyright, SPAM, cache and privacy regulations.* New York: John Wiley & Sons.

Davidson, Hall. (1999). The educator's lean and mean no fat guide to fair use. *Technology and Learning, 20*(2), 58–64.

Ercegovac, Z., & Richardson, J. V. (2004, July). Academic dishonesty, plagiarism included in the digital age: A literature review. *College and Research Libraries, 65*(4), 301–318.

Ferelli, Mark. (2000). Copyright in cyberspace: Unshaken but not unchanged. *Computer Technology Review, 20*(7), 6.

Fishman, D. (1999). Copyright in a digital world: Intellectual property rights in cyberspace. In S. J. Drucker & G. Gumpert (Eds.), *Real law@virtual space* (pp. 205–226). Cresskill, NJ: Hampton Press.

Fitzpatrick, Eileen. (2000, April 22). Metallica sues Napster & 3 universities. *Billboard, 112* (17), 3.

Fitzpatrick, Eileen. (2000, May 20). RIAA, Metallica wins Napster round, *Billboard, 112*(21), 8–9.

Halbert, Debora J. (1999). *Intellectual property in the information age: The politics of expanding ownership rights.* Westport, CN: Quorum.

Hansen, S. (2004, August 22). Dear plagiarists: You get what you pay for. *The New York Times Book Review,* 11.

Herbeck, D. A., & Hunter, C. D. (2001). Intellectual property in cyberspace. The use of protected images on the World Wide Web. *Communication Research Reports, 15*(1), 57–63.

Hinman, L. M. (2002, March). Academic integrity and the World Wide Web. *Computers and Society, 31*(1), 33–42.

Hinman, L. M. (2002, February). The impact of the Internet on our moral lives in America. *Ethics and Information Technology, 4*(1), 31–35.

Howard, R. M. (1999). *Standing in the shadow of giants: Plagiarists, authors, collaborators.* Stamford, CT: Ablex.

Kleinman, N. (1996). Don't fence me in: Copyright, property, and technology. In L. Strate, R. Jacobson, & S. Gibson (Eds.), *Communication and cyberspace* (pp. 59–82). Cresskill, NJ: Hampton Press.

Koepsell, David R. (2000). *The ontology of cyberspace: Philosophy, law and the future of intellectual property.* Chicago: Open Court Publishing.

Lessig, L. (2004). *Free culture: How big media uses technology and the law to lock down culture and control creativity.* New York: Penguin Books.

Litman, J. (2001). *Digital copyright.* Amherst, NY: Prometheus Books.

Moscou, Jim. (1999). Copyright in the digital age. *Editor and Publisher, 132*(50), 32, 34.

Pedzich, Joan. (2001, May 15). Protecting your company's intellectual property: A practical guide to trademarks, copyrights, patents and trade secrets. *Library Journal, 126*(9), 144.

Poynder, Richard. (1999). What price copyright? *Information Today, 16*(11), 14–17.

Renard, L. (1999/2000). Cut and paste 101: Plagiarism and the net. *Educational Leadership, 57,* 38–42.

Scanlon, P. M. (2002). Student online plagiarism: How do we respond? *College Teaching, 51*(4), 161–165.

Scanlon, P. M., & Neumann, D. R. (2002). Internet plagiarism among college students. *Journal of College Student Development, 43*(3), 374–385.

Snapper, J. W. (1999). On the Web, plagiarism matters more than copyright piracy. *Ethics and Information Technology, 1,* 127–136.

Winston, Paul D. (2000). Copying this article is strictly prohibited. *Business Insurance, 34*(36), 21.

Young, J. R. (2001, July 6). The cat-and-mouse game of plagiarism detection. *Chronicle of Higher Education,* A26–A27.

When and How to Cite Web Sources

CITATION STYLES

Citation styles generally fall into two categories: *humanities*—for example, Modern Language Association (MLA) or Chicago; or *scientific*—for example, American Psychology Association (APA) or Council of Biology Editors (CBE). These manuals list how to do both print and electronic sources. Here we'll be focusing on the online or electronic citations.

Scientific Style (APA or CBE)

For the most part, articles in online publications for the sciences are exact duplicates of the print versions. They are not likely to have additional analysis or charts, and so on. Therefore, APA recommends that when citing the online version of an article, use the same basic primary print journal reference. If you have viewed the article only in its electronic form, add in brackets after the article title [Electronic version]. Here's an example:

> Szabo, J., Underwood, J. (2004). Cybercheats: Is Information and Communication Technology fuelling academic dishonesty? [Electronic version]. *Active Learning in Higher Education,* 5(2), 180–199.

If you have reason to believe that the online article differs in some way from its paper counterpart or that it includes additional data, you need to add the date on which you retrieved the document and the URL.

> Szabo, J., Underwood, J. (2004). Cybercheats: Is Information and Communication Technology fuelling academic dishonesty? *Active Learning in Higher Education,* 5(2), 180–199. Retrieved December 5, 2004, from http://alh.sagepub.com/cgi/reprint/5/2/180

There have been some significant changes to both APA and MLA citation styles for electronic resources in the most recent editions of these style manuals (APA 5th edition, 2001 and MLA 6th edition, 2003). Be sure to check these recent editions for additional information. See the bibliography at the end of this chapter for more information.

Humanities Style (MLA or Chicago)

MLA recommends using the citation style for print periodicals, modifying them as appropriate to the electronic source. MLA format always includes the date of access and the relevant URL.

> Pierce, Patricia. "The Great Shakespeare Fraud." <u>History Today</u> 54.5(2004): 4–6. <www.historytoday.com/54/5/pierce.html>.

MLA recommends the use of angle brackets (< >) around any URL in type. The idea is to avoid confusion about where the URL begins and ends.

CITING ONLINE NEWSPAPER ARTICLES

SCIENTIFIC STYLE

Newspaper articles from a subscription-based database (e.g., ProQuest, Newsbank, or Lexis-Nexis)

> Author Last name, First initial. (year, Month day). Article title. *Newspaper Title,* page number. Retrieved month day, year, from database name.

> *Example*
> Haurwitz, R. K. M. (2004, December 6). UT in Rose Bowl? Not quite priceless, but pretty pricey. *Austin American-Statesman,* p. A8. Retrieved December 7, 2004, from Lexis-Nexis Academic Universe.

Newspaper articles from a website (e.g., the newspaper's website) on the Internet

> Author Last name, First initial. (year, Month day). Article title. *Newspaper Title,* page number. Retrieved month day, year, from URL.

> *Example*
> McLemee, S. (2004, September 24). 2 Cases of plagiarism, and an explanation of why the practice might be worth it. *Chronicle of Higher Education.* Retrieved December 7, 2004, from www.chronicle.com

HUMANITIES STYLE

Newspaper articles from a subscription-based database (e.g., ProQuest, Newsbank, or Lexis-Nexis) on the Internet

> Author Last name, First name. "Article Title." <u>Newspaper Title.</u> day Month year: page numbers. <u>Database Name</u> (if known). Name of Service (if known). Date of access day month year <url>.

> *Example*
> Haurwitz, Ralph K. M. "UT in Rose Bowl? Not Quite Priceless, but Pretty Pricey." <u>Austin American-Statesman.</u> 6 December 2004:A8. <u>Academic Universe</u> Lexis-Nexis. 7 December 2004, <http://web lexis-nexis.com/universe>.

Newspaper articles from a website (e.g., the newspaper's website) on the Internet

> Author Last name, First name. "Article Title." <u>Newspaper Title.</u> day Month year. date retrieved day Month year <url>.

> *Example*
>
> McLemee, Scott. "2 Cases of Plagiarism, and an Explanation of Why the Practice Might be Worth It." <u>Chronicle of Higher Education.</u> 24 September 2004. 7 December 2004 <www.chronicle.com>.

CITING ONLINE MAGAZINE ARTICLES

Generally, the terms "magazine" and "journal" are interchangeable. However, when it comes to scholarly writing and citing your sources, there is a difference. Journals are of a scholarly nature. Journal articles are in depth, and are often reviewed in depth by experts before being accepted for publication by the journal editors. Articles may be peer reviewed or, more rigorously, blind reviewed: a process whereby reviewers do not know who the author is and the author does not know who the reviewers are. Magazines feature articles on more popular topics that go into less depth and are usually written in a lighter style that is easy to read.

SCIENTIFIC STYLE

Magazine articles from a subscription database on the Internet

> Author Last name, First initial. (Year, Month day). Article title. *Magazine Title, volume*(issue)[if given], pages. Retrieved month day, year, from database name.

> *Example*
>
> King, P. (2004, December 6). A real stretch. *Sports Illustrated,* 101(22), 24–26. Retrieved December 7, 2004, from Academic Search Premier.

Magazine articles from a website (e.g., the magazine's website) on the Internet

> Author Last name, First initial. (Year, Month day). Article title. *Magazine Title, volume*(issue)[if given], pages. Retrieved Month day, year, from URL

Example

Hennen, T. (2004, October). Great American public libraries: The 2004 HAPLR rankings, *American Libraries,* 54–59. Retrieved December 7, 2004, from www.ala.org

HUMANITIES STYLE

Magazine articles from a subscription database on the Internet

Author Last name, First name. "Article Title." <u>Magazine Title.</u> day Month year: page numbers. <u>Database Name</u> (if known). Name of Service (if known). Date of access day Month year <url>.

Example

King, Peter. "A Real Stretch," <u>Sports Illustrated.</u> December 6, 2004:24–26. <u>Academic Search Premier.</u> EBSCO. December 7, 2004, <http://web34.epnet.com>.

Magazine articles from a website (e.g., the magazine's website) on the Internet

Author Last name, First name. "Article Title." <u>Magazine Title.</u> article day Month year. access day month year <url>.

Example

Hennen, Thomas. "Great American Public Libraries: The 2004 HAPLR Rankings." <u>American Libraries.</u> October 2004. December 7, 2004 <www.ala.org>.

CITING ONLINE JOURNALS

SCIENTIFIC STYLE

Journal articles from a subscription database on the Internet

Author Last name, First initial. (Year). Article title. *Journal Title, volume*(issue)[if given], pages. Retrieved Month day, year, from database name.

Example

Walther, J. (2004). Language and communication technology. *Journal of Language and Social Psychology, 23*(4), 384–396. Retrieved December 8, 2004, from ArticleFirst database.

Journal articles from a website (e.g., the journal's website) on the Internet

Author Last name, First initial. (Year, Month [if needed]). Article title. *Journal Title, volume*(issue)[if given], pages. Retrieved month day, year, from URL

Example

Booth, F. W., Chakravarthy, M. V., Gordon, S. E., & Spangenburg, E. E. (2002, July). Waging war on physical inactivity: Using modern molecular ammunition against an ancient enemy. *Journal of Applied Physiology, 93*(1), 3–30. Retrieved September 29, 2003, from http://jap.physiology.org/cgi/content/full/93/1/3

HUMANITIES STYLE

Journal articles from a subscription database on the Internet

Author Last name, First name. "Article Title." <u>Journal Title.</u> volume.issue (year): page numbers. <u>Database Name</u> (if known). Name of Service (if known). Date of access day Month year <url>.

Example

Walther, Joseph. "Language and Communication Technology." <u>Journal of Language and Social Psychology,</u> 23.4 (2004) 384–396. <u>ArticleFirst.</u> OCLC. 8 December 2004 <http://bulldogs.tlu.edu:2056/dbname=ArticleFirst;done=referer;FSIP>.

Journal articles from a website (e.g., the journal's website) on the Internet

Author Last name, First name. "Article Title." <u>Journal Title.</u> volume.issue(year): pp. number of pages. access day Month year <url>.

Example

Booth, Frank W., Chakravarthy, Manu V., Gordon, Scott E., & Spangenburg, Espen E. (2002). "Waging War on Physical Inactivity:

Using Modern Molecular Ammunition Against an Ancient Enemy."
Journal of Applied Physiology, 93.1:pp. 27. 29 September 2003
<http://jap.physiology.org/cgi/content/full/93/1/3>.

CITING ONLINE BOOKS

SCIENTIFIC STYLE

Author Last name, First initial. (year of publication). *Book title.* Place
of publication: Publisher. Retrieved Month day year. from URL

Example

Lawrence, B. (2004). *Real Indians and others: Mixed-blood urban
native peoples and indigenous nationhood.* Lincoln: University of
Nebraska Press. Retrieved October 3, 2004 from www.netlibrary.com/
Default.aspx

HUMANITIES STYLE

Author Last name, First name. Book Title. Ed. [editor's name if needed].
Place of publication: Publisher, publication date of original print
version [if given]. Internet site. Date of access day Month year <URL>.

Example

Lawrence, Bonita. Real Indians and Others: Mixed-blood Urban Native
Peoples and Indigenous Nationhood. Lincoln: University of Nebraska
Press, 2004. Netlibrary. 3 October 2004 <www.netlibrary.com/
Default.aspx>.

CITING DISCUSSION LIST ENTRIES

SCIENTIFIC STYLE

Author Last name, First initial. (year, Month day). Subject of message.
Message posted to name of list, archived at URL

Example

Barr, L. (2000, August 29). Call number dates for UMI reprinted
dissertations. Message posted to Autocat, archived at
http://listserv.acsu.buffalo.edu/archives/autocat.html

HUMANITIES STYLE

Author Last name, First name. "subject of message." Online posting. [date of posting] day Month year. List name. [date of access] day month year <URL of archives>.

Example

Barr, Linda. "Call number dates for UMI reprinted dissertations." Online posting 29 August 2000. Autocat. 3 September 2000 <http://listserv.acsu.buffalo.edu/archives/autocat.html>.

CITING EMAIL MESSAGES

SCIENTIFIC STYLE

In APA's most recent (5th) edition email communications from individuals should be considered as personal communications. Personal communications are not cited in the reference list: For more information see the APA manual, listed in the bibliography at the end of this chapter.

HUMANITIES STYLE

Author Last name, First name. "Subject." email to [recipient]. Day Month year.

Example

Radford, Marie. "Status of project." email to Linda Barr. 25 July 2000.

CITING GOVERNMENT RESOURCES

In the summer of 2000, the U.S. Government Printing Office (GPO) stated that web-only versions of previously printed documents produced by and for government agencies would begin to be published. The GPO is rapidly phasing out the costly printing of government documents in favor of delivering them electronically whenever possible. As you might imagine, the U.S. government puts out an incredible amount of information each year. (For example, think about the amount of information distributed by the Bureau of the Census, the IRS, the U.S. Congress, and our court systems.) This radical change in the way our government is distributing information makes it important to understand how to cite these electronic documents.

Government publications are written by or for federal agencies and printed, not published, by the GPO. These publications do not follow a standard title page arrangement, whether on paper or online. The basic form of a document retrieved via online databases or the Internet should include the author, title and edition, date of publication, date of retrieval, database and URL.

SCIENTIFIC STYLE

Author. (Publication date). *Title*. (Publication No. [if needed]). Retrieved Month day, year, from database name: URL

Example

U.S. General Accounting Office. (1997, February). *Telemedicine: Federal strategy is needed to guide investments*. (Publication No. GAO/NSAID/HEHS-97–67). Retrieved December 7, 2004, from General Accounting Office Reports Online via GPO Access: www.gpoaccess.gov/gaoreports/search.html

HUMANITIES STYLE

Name of the government. Name of agency. Title. By Author [if available]. [Date of publication] day Month year. [Date of access] day month year <URL>.

Example

United States. Dept. of Justice. Office of Juvenile Justice and Delinquency Prevention. Law Enforcement and Juvenile Crime. By Howard N. Snyder. Dec. 2001. 29 June 2002 <www.ncjrs.org/pdffiles1/ojjdp/191031.pdf>.

CITING A WEB PAGE

NOTE: When an Internet document is more than one web page, provide a URL that links to the home page or entry page for the document.

SCIENTIFIC STYLE

Author Last name, First initial. (Date of publication). *Title/name of article/web page.* Retrieved Month date, year, from URL

Example

Turner, T. (2004). *Coral Reef Ecology Home Page.* November 24, 2004, from www.uvi.edu/coral.reefer/

HUMANITIES STYLE

Title of site. Ed. Name of editor [if needed]. Year [date of electronic publication or of the latest update]. Sponsoring organization [if needed]. [date of access] day Month year <URL>

Example

The Coral Reef Ecology Home Page. Turner, Teresa. 2004. University of the Virgin Islands. 24 November 2004 <www.uvi.edu/coral.reefer/>

SUMMARY

In this chapter you read about

- How to cite web resources using citation formats for both humanities and scientific styles
- How to cite online newspaper articles
- How to cite online magazine articles
- How to cite online journal articles
- How to cite discussion list entries
- How to cite email messages
- How to cite online government resources
- How to cite a web page

WEB RESOURCES

American Psychological Association Recommended Electronic Reference Formats
www.apastyle.org/elecref.html

APA Citation Style, Long Island University, B. Davis Schwartz Memorial Library
www.liunet.edu/cwis/cwp/library/ workshop/citapa.htm

Columbia Guide to Online Style (CGOS)
www.columbia.edu/cu/cup/cgos/ idx_basic.html

Frequently Asked Questions about MLA Style
www.mla.org/style_faq

Internet Public Library, Citing Electronic Resources
www.ipl.org/div/farq/netciteFARQ.html

Online Citation Styles Index
www.bedfordstmartins.com/online/citex.html

Style Sheets for Citing Resources (Print & Electronic): Examples & General Rules for MLA, APA, Chicago & Turabian
www.lib.berkeley.edu/TeachingLib/Guides/ Internet/Style.html

Uncle Sam—Brief Guide to Citing Government Publications
exlibris.memphis.edu/resources/unclesam/ citeweb.html

BIBLIOGRAPHY FOR FURTHER READING

The Bluebook: A uniform system of citation (16th ed.). (1997). Cambridge: Harvard Law Review Association.

Chicago manual of style (15th ed.). (2003). Chicago: University of Chicago Press.

Council of Biology Editors. *Scientific style and format: The CBE manual for authors, editors, and publishers* (6th ed.). (1994). NY: Cambridge University Press.

Gibaldi, Joseph. (2003). *MLA handbook for writers of research papers* (6th ed). New York: Modern Language Association of America.

Gibaldi, Joseph. (2003). *MLA style manual and guide to scholarly publishing* (6th ed.). New York: Modern Language Association of America.

Publication manual of the American Psychological Association (5th ed.). (2001). Washington, DC: American Psychological Association.

Walker, Janice, & Taylor, Todd. (1998). *Columbia guide to online style.* New York: Columbia University Press.

● ●

Anchors.   Linked points on the same web page.

AND operator.   A Boolean operator used to *narrow* searches. When used in web searches, *AND* requires that both terms be present to be retrieved. For example, *math **AND** calculus* only returns sites with both terms.

Banner ads.   Advertisements placed on web pages that often appear as long horizontal boxes placed at the top of a page.

Bibliography.   A list of references and/or additional readings usually located at the end of a research paper.

Blog (also, web log).   An online web diary, usually devoted to a specific topic, generally providing links to related sites. Some blogs allow comments to be added by visitors. Range from personal experiences to general commentaries on current news.

Boolean operators.   The words AND, OR, or NOT (always capitalized) that can be used to construct search strategies. The most common Boolean operators are AND, OR, and NOT. These connect the terms you are searching and are used to narrow or broaden a search. For example, child AND violence, narrows your search to mean that you are looking for articles or web pages including both terms; child OR children broadens your search to mean that you are looking for articles or web pages including either term; violence NOT television narrows your search to mean that you want to exclude articles or web pages containing the second term.

Browsers.   Programs that interpret and display documents formatted in the hypertext markup language (HTML).

Citation.   Bibliographic information about a particular document. Generally citations include the author, title, publisher, place of publication, and date. Citations for web resources also include additional elements, such as the URL and date accessed.

Citation style.   A proscribed method of ordering the elements of a citation. Common citation styles include MLA (Modern Language Association), APA (American Psychological Association), and Chicago styles.

Copyright.   The exclusive right to sell, publish, or distribute a creative work or intellectual property.

Creative Commons Licensing. An alternative to traditional copyright law. This is a more flexible copyright license that allows the author of a work to choose the type of restrictions that they want to place on their original content. Under this licensing, content is marked by a CC instead of a copyright mark.

DMCA. Acronym for Digital Millenium Copyright Act.

Domain names. Names that identify the type of organization operating the Internet server. The five generic domains are gov, edu, com, net, and org. Additionally, domain names can include country codes, for example *ca* for Canada and *us* for United States.

Extensions. The three letters added to a file name to indicate the type of file. At the end of Internet URL addresses extensions refer to the Internet domain name, for example, .com = commercial, .net = host or gateway, .edu = educational organization, .gov = governmental, .org = nonprofit organization.

External links. Internet links that connect pages from different websites.

False hit (also, false drop). A site returned by a search engine that is not relevant to your search topic. This situation is common with keyword searches, especially when the keyword has more than one meaning. For example, you may be looking for information about JAVA, the programming language. You type in the term *JAVA*. The search engine returns a list of sites, including those about the programming language JAVA (*hits*), but also those about the Indonesian country (*false hits*) and even sites that have the term JAVA used as a slang term for coffee (*false hits*).

Flash Drive (also, USB drive). The USB Flash Drive is a portable storage device for computer equipped with a USB port. These devices plug directly into your USB port on any compatible computer and can support up to 2GB disk space. USB Drives are "plug and play" compatible devices.

Freedom of Information Act (FOIA). A law that states every federal executive-branch agency must publish instructions on how the public should get information from their agency.

Gator. A software product that places pop-up ads in other people's websites. Often these are advertisements for competitive products.

Graphical user interfaces (GUIs). The use of icons instead of typed commands to execute computer instructions. This type of interface design uses windows, pull-down menus, visual metaphors (such as the desktop), and a mouse. The two major GUIs are Windows and Macintosh.

Hate speech.   Making racist or discriminatory comments on the basis of race, gender, origin, disability or sexual orientation.

Hyperlink.   Usually called links, these are areas of the web page that are linked or connected to a different page or part of the same page. Selecting a link will take you to a different piece of information. Links can be images, words, pictures, or phrases.

Hypertext.   Nonsequential reading and writing. Information is connected or linked together and viewed in an associative way instead of as a linear sequence.

Hypertext markup language (HTML).   Codes used to format World Wide Web documents. Individual codes define the hierarchy and nature of the various components of the document, and specify hypertext links. For example, <title>Title</title> would show the title of a Web document or page.

Hypertext transport protocol (HTTP).   A communication protocol designed for web browsers that allows users to move from web page to web page around the World Wide Web.

Integrated search engines.   Search engines that run searches on multiple search engines and return an integrated list of sites displayed in a single list with duplicates removed.

Intellectual property.   The creative work of an individual or groups of individuals, including the creation of written work, artwork, and software programs.

Internal links.   Internet links that connect pages within a website.

Meta–search engines.   Search engines that run searches on other search engines and directories. Can return results that are integrated (sites displayed in a single list with duplicate sites removed) or nonintegrated (sites displayed in separate lists with duplicate sites remaining).

Metasites (also, subject directories).   Collections of high-quality web pages organized into subject categories, usually by human indexers who are librarians or subject specialists.

Misinformation.   On the Internet, misinformation is providing false or erroneous information as a means of deliberate deception or technological glitches.

Nonintegrated search engines.   Search engines that run searches on multiple search engines and return a list of sites displayed in separate lists with duplicate sites remaining.

NOT operator. A Boolean operator used for *exclusion*. When used in web searches, *NOT* requires that one term not be present. For example, *math* **NOT** *calculus* returns sites with the term *math*, but not the term *calculus*.

Online journalism. The use of the Internet as a reporting tool for stories distributed through traditional media; or the Internet can be used as a medium for news distribution.

OR operator. A Boolean operator used to *broaden* searches. When used in web searches, *OR* requires that either term be present to be retrieved. For example, *math* **OR** *mathematics* returns sites with either term or both terms.

Plagiarism. Using someone else's ideas and words without providing the proper citations or references.

Portal sites. Web traffic control sites that are designed to attract users before they visit other sites on the Internet. They provide gateways to accessing Internet information.

Precision. A measure of the effectiveness of your search. How many on-target/on-topic sites did the search engine find in relation to the total number of sites found?

Push technology. Technology that enables advertising messages to be pushed onto web users. This is often done through pop-up windows and animated banner advertisements.

Relevance. The degree to which the sites you found are judged by you to be on target, that is, actually about your topic.

Search engines. Software tools that allow web users to find information on the network. Presently, search engines are text based, and information is located through key word searches.

Subject directory. See *Metasites*.

Uniform Resource Locator (URL). The address that defines the route to a file on the Web or any other Internet facility. URLs are typed into the browser to access web pages, and URLs are embedded within the pages themselves to provide the hypertext links to other pages. For example, www.ablongman.com is a URL.

Universal usability. The ability of more than 90 percent of all households to successfully use information and communication technologies at least once a week.

USB drive.   See *Flash drive.*

Visual hierarchy.   A group of visual (and verbal) elements arranged according to emphasis. Emphasis is achieved with contrast, stressing the relative importance, separation, or connection of graphic elements.

Web rings.   Sites with a common interest that band together into linked circles to enable people to find them more quickly and easily.

Index